Praise for Dr. Dragos and
The Pursuit of Dreams

"In this engaging book, Dr. Dragos Bratasanu shows us that science is the contemporary language of spirituality. Read it, and you will learn that everything in your life is an initiation to your true potential—and pain and suffering, when you apply your will to move through difficult experiences, is the birthing process of wisdom. The Pursuit of Dreams teaches us that when we trust ourselves and fully surrender, our dreams will come true."

— **Dr. Joe Dispenza**, *New York Times* best-selling author of *Becoming Supernatural* and *You Are the Placebo*

"The Pursuit of Dreams is the container for an elegant code. It's an advanced and consciousness-shifting 'mind-ware' that can breathe life into your greatest dreams and life's passions."

— **Gregg Braden**, *New York Times* best-selling author of *Human by Design* and *The Divine Matrix*

"Dr. Dragos stands for the hopeless, for the ones who starve for more meaning and purpose, for the rejected and the lonely. The genius of Dr. Dragos makes us clearly see that beyond our suffering, doubts, and problems that we face in life, there is a place in our hearts where courage, hope, and love still make our dreams possible."

— **Guy Djoken**, CEO and executive director of UNESCO Center for Peace

THE PURSUIT OF DREAMS

Hay House Titles of Related Interest

YOU CAN HEAL YOUR LIFE, the movie,
starring Louise Hay & Friends
(available as a 1-DVD program, an expanded
2-DVD set, and an online streaming video)
Learn more at www.hayhouse.com/louise-movie

THE SHIFT, the movie,
starring Dr. Wayne W. Dyer
(available as a 1-DVD program, an expanded
2-DVD set, and an online streaming video)
Learn more at www.hayhouse.com/the-shift-movie

***

*BECOMING SUPERNATURAL: How Common People
Are Doing the Uncommon,* by Dr. Joe Dispenza

*CHOICES AND ILLUSIONS: How Did I Get Where I Am,
and How Do I Get Where I Want to Be?* by Eldon Taylor

*THE MOTIVATION MANIFESTO: 9 Declarations
to Claim Your Personal Power,* by Brendon Burchard

*RESILIENCE FROM THE HEART:
The Power to Thrive in Life's Extremes,* by Gregg Braden

*SHIFT HAPPENS! How to Live an Inspired Life . . .
Starting Right Now!* by Robert Holden, Ph.D.

All of the above are available at your local bookstore,
or may be ordered by visiting:

Hay House USA: www.hayhouse.com®
Hay House Australia: www.hayhouse.com.au
Hay House UK: www.hayhouse.co.uk
Hay House India: www.hayhouse.co.in

THE PURSUIT OF DREAMS

CLAIM YOUR POWER, FOLLOW YOUR HEART, AND FULFILL YOUR DESTINY

DR. DRAGOS BRATASANU

HAY HOUSE, INC.
Carlsbad, California • New York City
London • Sydney • Johannesburg
Vancouver • New Delhi

Published and distributed in the United States by: Hay House, Inc.: www.hayhouse.com® • **Published and distributed in Australia by:** Hay House Australia Pty. Ltd.: www.hayhouse.com.au • **Published and distributed in the United Kingdom by:** Hay House UK, Ltd.: www.hayhouse.co.uk • **Distributed in Canada by:** Raincoast Books: www.raincoast.com • **Published in India by:** Hay House Publishers India: www.hayhouse.co.in

Cover design: Christopher Tobias, tobiasdesign.com
Interior design: Howie Severson

Library of Congress Cataloging-in-Publication Data

Names: Bratasanu, Dragos, date, author.
Title: The pursuit of dreams : claim your power, follow your heart, and fulfill your destiny / Dr. Dragos Bratasanu.
Description: Carlsbad : Hay House, Inc., 2018.
Identifiers: LCCN 2017050492 | ISBN 9781401952600 (paperback)
Subjects: LCSH: Self-actualization (Psychology) | Happiness. | Success. | BISAC: BODY, MIND & SPIRIT / New Thought. | BODY, MIND & SPIRIT / Inspiration & Personal Growth. | SELF-HELP / Personal Growth / Happiness. | SELF-HELP / Personal Growth / Success.
Classification: LCC BF637.S4 B688 2018 | DDC 158--dc23 LC record available at https://lccn.loc.gov/2017050492

ISBN: 978-1-4019-5260-0

10 9 8 7 6 5 4 3 2 1
1st edition, April 2018

SUSTAINABLE FORESTRY INITIATIVE
Certified Chain of Custody
Promoting Sustainable Forestry
www.sfiprogram.org
SFI-01268
SFI label applies to the text stock

Printed in the United States of America

To Anca

CONTENTS

PART III WALK IN TRUTH

FOREWORD

The book you're about to explore is more than a collection of amazing stories and powerful life lessons! *The Pursuit of Dreams* is the container for an elegant code. It's an advanced and consciousness-shifting "mind-ware" that can breathe life into your greatest dreams and passions. Through an easy read that's just the right mix of adventure and intimate biography, Dragos Bratasanu shares the story of his life in Eastern Europe and the pursuit of his passion until his heartfelt dreams replaced the struggle he'd known in his past. And this is where the magic begins!

As your eyes absorb the words, they spark the dance of light in your brain that opens the floodgate to your most empowering beliefs. It's at this crossroads, where our own consciousness interacts with another person's experience, that we shift our idea of what's possible in our lives. And when we do, we set into motion the brain shift necessary to make our own dreams come true. It's all based upon rock-solid science. Here's what I mean.

THE POWER OF SEEING THE IMPOSSIBLE

On July 26, 1852, British sprinter Charles Westhall accomplished something that was thought to be impossible at the time. Running in a torrential downpour on a race-track in London, Westhall set the official time for running one mile at a stunning 4 minutes and 28 seconds. And although his record would be broken 31 more times in the late 1800s and early 1900s, each new record was only slightly better than the original time. All fell short of breaking the elusive four-minute mark for running a mile. For over 100 years, it was thought—*it was believed and accepted*—that four minutes is the limit to how fast a human can run a mile. It was known that our bones and muscles are simply not built to carry our bodies any faster. That is, until the impossible happened on May 6, 1954.

On that day, for the first time in history, British runner Roger Bannister broke the "impossible" four-minute barrier for running a mile. Bannister clocked his paradigm-shattering run at a blazing 3 minutes and 59.4 seconds. And this is where the story of the four-minute mile illustrates the theme of this book. Although it took 102 years for Bannister to break the original 1852 record for the four-minute mile, once he did so, it took only *46 days* for that record to be broken *again*. This time it was broken by Australian runner John Landy in a run of 3 minutes and 57.9 seconds. Not only had the "impossible" four-minute mile been shattered, it was shattered twice in less than seven weeks!

When we read about Roger Bannister's record mile and how that record was broken time and again, the question is this: What changed to make the new records possible? The length of the mile didn't change—it was still the official 5,280 feet. The bodies of the runners didn't change—they were still training, eating, and practicing just as they had the year before. The factor that *did change* is what the runners believed about the mile itself and their relationship to it. It was only after this powerful shift in thinking was in place that the athletes could accomplish their dreams of being the fastest humans on earth.

THE KEY

For us to accept that something is possible in our life, we need a catalyst to shift our thinking—a reason to believe that something is possible. So when the barrier of a four-minute mile was breached for the first time and the extraordinary feat was witnessed by other runners, such a reason was provided. And once it was clear that a human could, in fact, run a mile in less than four minutes, the emotional code was unleashed for other people to do the same thing. The record was broken time after time, with some of the records being broken by the same people who had set them previously!

I'm sharing the history of the four-minute mile to illustrate a powerful principle of human potential. The key that made it possible to break Roger Bannister's record is this: when we experience someone else accomplishing what we once believed to be impossible—*either visually or through the written word*—it frees us to do the same thing . . . and even more.

Once we accept and embrace that something is possible for us, we set into motion a cascade of emotional and physiological processes in our body that support our acceptance. This is how we transcend the limits of our past and realize our maximum human potential. A recent scientific discovery tells us precisely how this principle works and the potential it holds for our lives.

WHEN WITNESSING IS EXPERIENCING

In 2004, Italian scientists published the results of a research project describing why Roger Bannister's record-breaking run had such a powerful effect on other runners. The discovery, published in *The Annual Review of Neuroscience*, was the existence of specialized cells in the brain called mirror neurons.

A mirror neuron fires in response to two very different kinds of experiences:

- when we have an experience for ourselves
- when we *witness* someone else having an experience

In other words, the discovery revealed that our brain doesn't know the difference between watching someone having an experience and living the same experience! But we don't need a research paper to tell us this. Even without a technical understanding of the mechanism, we experience the power of mirror neurons frequently—for example, when we're watching a Sunday afternoon football or soccer game at home.

Although we might be on a chair or sofa in our living room, almost motionless, our body is anything but calm. Sports spectators commonly experience symptoms as if they're the ones actually playing the game, such as an elevated heart rate, tense muscles, rapid breathing, and perspiring. Even though we're watching from the comfort of our home, to our mirror neurons we may as well be on the playing field.

When we watch, witness, or read something we identify with emotionally, our brains are releasing the same powerful chemicals, such as adrenaline, endorphins, dopamine and serotonin, that they would if we were actually experiencing what we're seeing or reading about. The discovery of mirror neurons explains why *The Pursuit of Dreams* is such a powerful book and reveals the potential that it holds for your life today.

When you read Dr. Bratasanu's journey of discovery, your mirror neurons fire as if *you* are the one having the experience—as if you're the one breaking barriers, shattering perceptions, and living the dreams for yourself. This is the power of the pages that follow—they invite you beyond the limits of *your* personal past through experiencing the story of a person transcending the limits of *their* past.

THE POWER OF YOUR DREAM

Everybody has a dream. Some of us have huge dreams to change the world on a massive scale. And some of us simply dream of finding another person to love and accept us the way we long for within ourselves. Regardless of the magnitude, our dreams and the beliefs they're based upon influence everything from our choices of romance, life partners, and the most intimate moments of our lives to the way we solve our problems, the careers we choose, and matters of health, life, and death.

So, while we all dream, the question is: how do we awaken our most heartfelt dreams and make them a reality in our lives? *The Pursuit of Dreams* is the account of Dragos Bratasanu's journey to do just that. How did he do it? The answer is waiting for you in the pages that follow.

— Gregg Braden
New York Times best-selling author of
Human by Design and *The Divine Matrix*

O Father,
Thy will be done.

A NOTE FROM THE AUTHOR

Dear friend,

Do you believe everyone deserves to make their dreams a reality? I do. And because you are holding this book in your hands now, I believe you think and feel the same way.

Are you familiar with the pain of having a dream and not knowing how to transform it into reality?

Have you had the suffocating experience of staying in a job that drains the very life out of you, yet you rationalize all the reasons why you cannot leave?

Do you have a dream but are afraid to take the leap into the unknown and pursue your passion?

Did you ever choose the comfortable misery of a secure job that meant nothing to you over the calling of your heart?

There were times in my life when I've answered yes to all these questions. I know firsthand all the thought and pain that go into making each of these decisions. But it doesn't need to be this way.

This book you are now reading is not about positivity. This book reveals the raw and naked truth about each one of us. It's about why and how you can make your dreams a reality—no matter where you start.

You might say, "But you don't know my situation . . ." So let me tell you a story.

I grew up during the last years of Communism in Eastern Europe. It was a time when the line "give us this day our daily bread" had a very literal meaning: families were entitled to only a loaf of bread each day. As a student, I lived on a budget of one hundred dollars a month for five years; it was all my parents could afford to keep me in school. Yet, in spite of every lack and dark circumstance, God hid great dreams in my heart, and he kept calling me again and again to discover them. I believe that you picked up this book because you probably feel there's more to life than the emptiness in your heart, the meaningless job, and living for the weekend. There is so much more.

On a day just like any other day, I took the first step toward my dreams. I took baby steps and dared a little bit more every day. The change was not immediate, but my life was gently transformed from dark to light, from death to life, from heartbreak to joy, from broken hopes to wishes fulfilled. One by one, with endless hours of work, my dreams started to become reality. If you don't believe in your dreams, either, don't worry; just read on.

From a near-failure of a student in university who struggled each year to pass his exams, I went straight to achieving my Ph.D. in the field of satellite-based intelligence and winning multiple awards for my innovations in the space industry. My research was published in leading scientific journals. I was nominated for the list of MIT's Innovators Under 35—a most prestigious recognition for "the brightest minds in Europe who are changing society" with their ideas. I am living proof that when God qualifies you, nobody can disqualify you. When God gives you a dream, no one can take it away from you unless *you* give it up.

My dreams grew together with me. In my mid-20s, I worked and studied with the most renowned leaders from NASA. I was the engineer and journalist of a Mars simulation mission that paved the way for future flights to the Red Planet. I traveled alone on two expeditions to the North and the South Pole. In the pages of this book, you will discover how I traveled to the Arctic and the Antarctic on nothing but a dream, and you will learn how to apply the same insights to make your own dreams a reality.

Later in life, my career thrived, and I got a big job in the corporate world. Driven by social pressures rather than following my spirit, I started focusing on worldly success rather than my dreams, and I became blind to the Truth. Despite how great my life seemed from the outside, my heart began screaming from within a golden cage, calling me to return to my dreams. Unfortunately, I failed to listen. I lost my soul.

I was doing everything I should, but nothing I truly *wanted* to. I sank into a deep depression. The emotional pain became unbearable. After several years of denying reality, I wrapped my degree in Bubble Wrap and stuck it in the closet, leaving my career in aerospace to do what mattered most to me: inspire people to make their dreams a reality. I needed to start again from scratch—and I did.

In the pursuit of my dreams, I wrote books, produced movies, and helped people around the world heal a fragment of their lives. But do not forget where I started from: a student in Eastern Europe, with no money and no connections. I fulfilled my dreams not because I had anything special on my side, but because I kept taking baby steps every day into the great unknown.

If you are willing to give your dreams a chance, this book will help you make them happen. Following your dreams means living in Truth. This may be the most obvious and yet, ironically, the hardest thing to do in this world.

Look within yourself for a moment and think on these questions:

- What is your heart's calling?

- What does your heart yearn to do?

- Do you live your life from love?

- Are you honest to God and yourself about who you are and about your dreams?

- Imagine standing before God, and he asks you, "Have you fulfilled your purpose in the world?" What would you answer?

The Truth in your heart is calling you to fulfill your destiny. Together, let's take just a baby step in the pursuit of your dreams today to reclaim your freedom and your life.

Even if your pockets are empty, go where your heart is fulfilled. When you claim your power and follow your heart, by the time you reach any obstacles you see off in the distance, they will have been removed for you.

Maybe you've built a career and are afraid to start again from scratch. Jesus asked, "For what shall it profit a man, if he shall gain the whole world, and lose his own soul?" (Mark 8:36). As a man who lost his soul once, I also ask you: What shall you profit if you have your career and all material possessions, but you deny your heart and lose yourself?

Nothing in this world will fulfill you and make you happy until you honor your spirit. As you'll learn in this book, you can find healing and a sense of purpose only when you live in Truth. You will never find meaning in living a lie. I will guide you into the deepest chambers of your heart, where you will find your spirit and the Truth. And when you embrace that Truth, rivers of freedom will gush forth from within you. Even if you must begin again from scratch to work on your dreams, you will do so with great power and abundant joy.

The goal of this book is not to give a straightforward accounting of who I am and what I have done, nor do I follow historical fact with strict academic accuracy. I've changed the names of most characters or shifted their location to protect their privacy. In some chapters, I merged two or three people into one character for the sake of storytelling. Some stories and dialogues are parables. However, every story is inspired by real life, and *all* the scientific facts and spiritual teachings are accurate. This book took 10 years to write, and while I don't seek the praise of anyone for my work, I am accountable first and foremost to God, then to the international scientific community for every word I wrote herein.

In Part I, each of the chapters reflect on a different episode in my life. In each one, the setting, the time period, and my companions will vary, but the conclusion is the same: you must think greater than the social environment and live in Truth if you want to fulfill your destiny. I hope these stories heal your life, cause you to pause and reflect on your own circumstances, and send you on the path of your dreams.

In Part II, I share the story of how I pursued my dreams of going to the North and South Poles, with nothing more than high hopes. My wish is that these words help remove some of the fears from your path and rekindle your dreams.

In Part III, I discuss the events that led me to create *The Amazing You* film and where I am today, then bring all the topics together to explain what it means for *you*.

You will shine because you are the light of the world, even if you don't know it yet. You will be joyful and empowered because you will return to Truth. You will know, maybe even for the first time, that whoever you are, wherever you are, you matter. I believe you deserve to make your dreams a reality, and this book will set you free to go do it.

I love you,
Dr. Dragos
Wellington, New Zealand

LIVE IN TRUTH

Truth is not a thought, not a word,
not a relationship between things, not a law.
Truth . . . gives Life to all.

— SAINT NIKOLAJ VELIMIROVIĆ

CHAPTER 1

NOBODY SMILES IN THIS TOWN ANYMORE

Lies became the norm; the false became reality.

July 1984. A Small Town in Eastern Europe.

1.

I came into the world in 1984, 10 minutes before midnight, in a small town in Romania. My father was away on business, and my mother was alone in the apartment when her water broke.

We lived in the same apartment for 18 years until I left for college, but my parents didn't really tell me much about their lives before I showed up. I often look at their photos from when they were young to try to know them a little better. They seem to have many friends, and my mom always has her arms around my dad's neck. I sometimes imagine the stories they lived but never shared with me: two beautiful strangers with flowers in their hair, hungry for freedom. They were young, in love with life and each other, but they grew up during the most terrible years of Communism in Eastern Europe. No matter how hard you try to tell a story from old photographs, the paper shows you only what it wants you to see; the Truth remains a mystery of the human heart.

After my parents were married, they moved to a small port town on the river Danube. The oldest part of the town was built in the 1400s and has the air of a quiet neighborhood in Paris. Half a century ago, the houses looked like giant wedding cakes: tall white buildings were adorned with sculpted roses at the windows, and wooden doors were decorated with stone maple leaves, carved miniature columns, ferns, and ocean waves. White and blue and purple flowers poured from boxes on the balconies. On Sunday mornings, people came out of their homes to take a stroll in the park and go to church. They dressed in their finery, like the bride and groom figurines usually adorning a wedding cake. In those days, people greeted one another, chatting and laughing in the streets.

Back then, people smiled in this town. By the time my parents were born, the Communist Party took over the country. People were forced out of their homes, and any who refused to move were thrown in jail. People left their farms and their animals, leaving behind a lifetime of work and a trail of tears. They were moved into blocks of flats built for this purpose. The buildings spread like tumors on the face of the land. They called them "matchboxes": gray concrete boxes, one on top of the other, each crammed with destitute souls.

In desperation, some people swam across the Danube River under the cover of the darkness of night, to death or to freedom. Only a few escaped to foreign lands and never looked back. Most were caught, then left to languish, forgotten, in underground prisons. Many were afraid to run, and so they stayed.

Those who knew how to build radio devices hid in their basements after dark, and tuned in to European stations to learn about the Western world. Local radio and TV programs played only Communist propaganda. If you believed their words, you'd think that you were in the best place in the world.

If heaven was created in perfect love, then Romania was built on perfect fear. If heaven is freedom, then my corner of the world was a dungeon most people didn't know they were in. They received an education, but they learned only what they needed to know to do their work. People were sent to work somewhere in the country but had no freedom to choose their way. They received an apartment and a salary, but could never leave the country. Back then, Romania was a jail of souls, and the mortal sin was their yearning for freedom. They had to honor their mother and father—and both of these were the Communist Party. They could have no other party before it, as there was none. They couldn't take the name of the party in vain, because if they said the wrong thing, they were locked up. Those who wrote poems, played songs, or taught students about freedom were arrested and found guilty.

In this environment, people learned to fear others and not trust anyone. They adapted to the social context. They slammed the doors of their minds from the inside and lived there alone. They didn't dare to express themselves. They sealed their creative spirit. They became mute to the Truth, to their dreams, and to the freedom they needed to thrive. They managed their words and behavior so they could survive the social environment. They locked the Truth away inside, and worked every day to ignore it and keep it hidden.

As the years passed, lies became the norm; the false became reality. Their minds were troubled by anxiety, and the lies they lived became their experience of life. Every day after work, people went down to the basements of their buildings, hid from sight, and drank their reality away. Truth rotted on the inside, and alcohol became the savior from pain.

Today, nobody smiles in this town anymore.

2.

The day of my birth, my mother packed her things and left for the emergency room by herself. I turned around in her womb and placed my feet against its walls so I wouldn't fall out. For 12 hours, I looked away from the light, away from the voices calling me to come out. Suddenly the ceiling above opened up. Two blue arms grabbed my legs and wrenched me outside. I screamed, but it didn't impress them.

My mom fell asleep with me on her chest. That night after her cesarean surgery, she put me close to her heart, and she's held me there ever since. My dad did the same.

I grew up and went to school in this town where nobody smiled. Other children laughed at my giant head, like a dandelion-seed head floating above a skinny body. My ears came folded, and my mother had to tie them to my head with a gauze bandage for several months; I looked like an elephant. When I tried to speak, I mumbled, moving and swapping the words in my mind as I tried to find the right order in which to say them.

I blinked constantly with my right eye, and the corner of my upper lip raised every other second without my permission. Eventually, this tic gave way to another, then another, and another. First, my upper lip fluttered, making me look like a confused dog, growling with gentle eyes. Then my lower lip dropped so low that my relatives thought I was drunk all the time. When my lips came back to normal, my mouth decided to smile every other second for no reason, but never with both corners at the same time. It was as if I were blinking with my lips. I thought I would never have a girlfriend.

In the first grade, our teacher told us that the mind has unseen powers, and that we could communicate with other people by thought alone. I had fallen in love with a girl in my classroom, but because I couldn't trust my face, I never said a word to her. I went home that day and decided to send her a message through my thoughts. I squeezed my eyes, clenched my hands, and tightened my body, trying to send her the thought that I liked her. My father walked in and asked me if I was trying to take a poop in bed.

I finally said good morning to that girl three days later, on the day I turned 10. Four years later, I summoned the courage to kiss her. Good things in life take time.

3.

The first years of my life were also the last, hardest years of Communism in Romania. My parents sacrificed their lives for me, but they could do only so much in our country. My mom worked in a bakery, and my dad labored in an industrial plant, striving six or seven days a week to make sure I had everything I needed.

Food became scarce. My grandparents had to stand in lines in front of grocery stores for hours before dawn to bring home a bottle of milk. The store shelves were empty after eight in the morning. Once a week, people could buy a few eggs and a slice of meat, controlled with food stamps by the authorities. The line "give us this day our daily bread" had literal meaning; my family was entitled to a loaf of bread each day and not much more. With every meal, my relatives reminded me how expensive food was. As they urged me to eat, they'd tell me the outrageous cost of chicken, tomatoes, cheese, and every morsel of food on my plate.

When I turned five, my parents took me to the only sweets shop in town. My eyes grew big, pupils dilating. My breath stopped. My taste buds danced. Rock 'n' roll played in my ears. My jaw dropped in a dumb smile when the bottle was placed on the table. "What is this drink and this color I've never seen before?" I asked my parents. *And why am I the only one at the table drinking it?* I thought to myself.

Pepsi-Cola was so rare in my country that you could find a bottle only if you came in at the right time, on a specific day of the month—*if* you were close friends with the owner of the store. My parents had talked him into hiding a bottle for me weeks before, but he didn't have another bottle for them. (Five more years passed until I had my first Coca-Cola.)

Like most children, I believed everything people around me ever told me. I believed them when they said life is hard. I believed we didn't have enough money. I believed that it was hard to get around these days. I believed the rich were criminals. I believed that people were hostile. I believed only others can be, do, or have what they want—but not me. I believed I was nobody, and I believed my only chance in life was to have good grades in school, but I also believed that I wasn't smart enough to achieve them. Eventually, I believed I wasn't enough.

It took 15 years for me to discover how the social environment creates our personal realities . . . and to realize how wrong I was about the way I perceived life and myself.

CHAPTER 2

ONE NIGHT IN TRANSYLVANIA WITH THE FATHER OF THE HUBBLE SPACE TELESCOPE

(PART 1)

When you listen and follow your heart,
you honor the spirit of God within you.

August 2013. Transylvania.

1.

I parked the car where the dirt road ended, at the top of the hill. The last sun rays of twilight caused the shadows of the cemetery stones to stretch across the pasture, like scrawny arms grasping for their escaping prey. People were already in their homes for the night, and only a horse-drawn carriage still scurried through the cornfields in the distance, chased by its long and growing shadow. Smoke rose through chimneys of homes in the valley, and the smell of burning wood blended with the fragrance of flowers to reach us up on the hill.

My friend Charlie and I still had a two-minute walk to get to the medieval church, but I wasn't sure we could get in. In the remote villages of Transylvania, priests lock their churches at sundown to protect them from thieves and vandals.

"I fell asleep in the car for a minute, and we've traveled hundreds of years back in time," said Charlie. "Where are we?"

"Let's walk. I want to show you one of the secret medieval churches in my country," I said. "Saint Nicholas in Densus is one of the oldest churches in Romania. Nobody knows who built it, but locals say that in ancient times, giants raised it on the ruins of a pagan temple."

"This is extraordinary," said Charlie when we walked through the gate. Grass had pierced through the rock floor in the churchyard, and parts of the wall had crumbled into piles of stones. Two painted saints, distressed by time, guarded the main door.

"For more than seven hundred years, people came here on Sundays to pray the gospel. They still do today," a gentle voice called out in heavily accented English. "Welcome to my church."

"Good evening, Father," I said, turning. "We didn't see you."

An old man appeared out of the shadows behind us. He was dressed in a black tunic, common among Christian orthodox priests in my country. His gray beard covered half of the wooden cross resting on his chest. A rosary and a rugged iron key chain swung from his hands. He walked with his head bowed, as if every step he took was a prayer. His eyes seemed to shine with a peace and light from beyond this world.

"We're glad you are here so late in the evening," I said. "My friend traveled all the way from America to visit Transylvania."

He passed us, iron keys jangling, and opened the door. "Come in," he told me in Romanian. "I will be at the altar. Feel free to look around and take pictures. No flash please. Close the door when you leave."

2.

Around us, the painted saints faded into the stone walls, washed away by the wear of hundreds of years. Charlie was reading the history of the place on the bulletin board, as I sat in a carved wooden chair next to the altar.

"What is your story, Father?" I asked the priest in Romanian. "What brought you to this remote place?"

"My dream had always been to serve God," he said. His eyes looked up to the painting of Jesus on the front wall. "When I was a kid, I used to pray in the secret of my room at night. I would rush home from school, close the door, and read from the Bible. When I woke up in the morning, the first words I said as I stretched in bed were 'Good morning, God.' I knew he was there with me. I could feel his presence and his love. Kids feel these things, you know?"

I nodded and smiled. He shone with kindness and serenity.

"I grew up," he continued, with a faint sadness in his voice. "My friends were not interested in God, and I never told them about my dream to become a pastor. We talked about music, girlfriends, and other people—everything else but our dreams. We made plans for college. I fell in love with a girl a few years older than me. She didn't know I existed, but I couldn't think of anything other than her for almost a year."

"I know how that feels. We've all had our hearts crushed, like a cigarette butt under a heel," I said.

"I spent less and less time with my books, and paid less attention to what really mattered to me. By the end of college, I had forgotten about God."

"But you have your church now . . ."

"I studied engineering. I worked for a decade for a software company. I lived in the city, and spent evenings with my friends, going to the gym or having drinks and chatting. Life was easy, but something was bothering me. There was an emptiness in my heart, and nothing seemed to fill it. It just wouldn't go away. This hollowness suffocated me, early in the morning after I woke up, and late in the evening before I fell asleep. Sundays were the worst."

"That's life for most of us," I said.

He continued. "When I turned thirty, a friend gave me a gift, a book on ancient spiritual traditions from around the world. I read during evenings and weekends. I read on the bus on my way to work. I read during lunch breaks. The stories and the parables, the photographs of ancient monasteries and sacred places, reminded me of my childhood and of my dream to become a minister.

"I traveled to a monastery in the mountains during weekends, and stayed in the garden for hours to listen to the sermon coming through the speakers. I took long walks in the park every day after work, and began talking to God when no one was looking. I walked in the cold pouring rain, when the park was deserted, and I could speak a little louder. I had forgotten how to pray, so I just told the truth and nothing but the truth—and God helped me. I just spoke from the bottom of my heart."

"You talked to God in the park?" I said.

"I didn't know it then, but yes, I did," he said. "The day I opened my heart and acknowledged the truth with my whole being, God answered my prayers and lifted the stone I'd crawled under. I felt free for the first time in ten years.

"As days passed, I noticed the emptiness in my heart faded when I was reading from the Bible and the books of the saints, or visiting the monastery during the weekend, but it became even more bitter when I was at work, writing software. The gap between what my heart called me to do and what I was actually doing grew until it became unbearable. I fell ill. I couldn't sleep, and I couldn't get out of bed for days. I knew what I had to do, but I didn't have the courage to do it."

I thought about his words for a moment. "I have friends who are going through similar experiences. They have a sense they want to do something new in life, but they are afraid to take the leap into the unknown. Their jobs seem to be draining the very life force out of them. They struggle with anxiety and depression; some battle addictions. Their health is failing."

He replied, "It took me thirty years to understand this mystery, son. If you want to know the truth and why this is happening to your friends, I will explain. I know because it also happened to me.

"Each one of us is God's house on earth. The spirit of God dwells within us. God put his spirit in our *hearts*; it is his spirit that gives us life. The spirit of God gives strength to our bodies, peace to our minds, and love to our hearts.

"Pay attention now because this one revelation can heal and transform your entire life. Jesus called the spirit of God the *Spirit of Truth*. Therefore, the life of God in our hearts *is* the Spirit of Truth. Life and Truth are one.

"The persistent calling in your heart to do something in life is the voice of God summoning you to fulfill your destiny. When you listen and follow your heart, you honor the spirit of God within you. Rivers of life gush forth from inside. You feel enthusiastic. In fact, the word *enthusiasm* comes from the Greek words *en*, meaning within, and *theos*, which means God; it literally translates as *God within*. When you honor the Spirit of Truth, your body is healed, your mind is sharp, and your heart is bathed in love. When you don't follow your heart and don't obey the Truth—the way I did for ten years when I worked as a software engineer in spite of my calling to become a pastor—you suppress the will of God within you.

"Of course, in your mind, you rationalize all the reasons why you can't fulfill your purpose. In fact, all you do is lie to yourself and repress the Truth. And where there are lies, the Spirit of Truth cannot abide. Because Truth and life are one, when you reject the Truth, you cut yourself off from the source of life. This is why people feel the life force draining out of them when they stay in jobs or relationships they don't want to be in—because it is. Removed from the source of life, your body becomes weak, your mind turns fearful, and your heart is empty and hollow."

"This all makes perfect sense to me," I said.

"The mystery goes even deeper. God is love; therefore, life and love and Truth are one. And for this reason, when you follow your heart and you honor the Truth, your entire life is filled with love."

"I guess my question is, what do we do?" I asked.

"You don't need anyone to tell you what to do. God has written your destiny in your heart. If you listen to his voice, you don't need anyone to teach you. This is not a figure of speech, but the simple reality. What do you love to do? Truth is always within you. Search your heart with all sincerity. Make sure everything is out in the light, and there's no deception in you. The painful emptiness we feel is the warning sign telling us to make our hearts true.

"Come to God with a pure heart, and find what he has prepared for you. Don't you know your dreams come from him? If you were to stand before God, and he asked you, 'Have you fulfilled your purpose in the world?'—what would you answer?

"Do not be afraid. God doesn't withdraw his call on your life, but you must listen to his voice."

3.

"Why did you wait ten years to pursue your dream?" I asked the pastor.

"I doubted and was afraid. I was telling others to trust God, but I was doing the opposite. I honored him with my lips, but dishonored him with my actions.

"To be honest with you, son, I felt I wasn't good enough to be a pastor. I was afraid of not being able to serve my community. I was afraid to give up my career and start from nothing one more time. I was a weak man, filled with fear about my life, and about the future."

In spite of the priest's somber words, his eyes shone with a peace that transcended my understanding. He continued, "On a Friday evening, I was walking home from the office, and stopped in front of the cathedral in the city square. The face of a friend I hadn't seen in years smiled at me from the bulletin board. He was holding an organ recital that evening. Next to his poster there was an old newspaper article called 'Letter from God to Man.'"

The father reached in his pocket and took out a rumpled piece of paper. He put his glasses on the tip of his nose and began reading:

I know your suffering. I know your inner conflicts, your struggles, and your pain. I know the sickness in your body, the doubts in your mind, and the fears in your heart. I know your weaknesses and your mistakes, and in spite of them all, I still ask you: give me your heart. Love me just the way you are. If you wait until you become an angel to love me, you will never love me. No matter how many mistakes you think you've made in the past, I still ask you to love me. Love me just the way you are.

I gave you a calling in life. Heed it just the way you are. If you wait until you don't make any more mistakes, you will never do it. I put a dream in your heart. If you wait until you believe you are ready, you will never pursue it. Follow your dream just the way you are. I gave you my life. Live your life in truth, or else you will never live it.

My child, I love you just the way you are. Of course, with time, I will transform your fear into love, your pain into joy, and your struggles into peace. But for now, love me just the way you are. Listen to your heart and answer my calling. I am Spirit, and I speak to your heart in love, in spirit, and in truth. My will is to see love rising even from the darkest corners of this world. I need your voice so I can speak through you. I need your hands to bring my gifts to all my sons and daughters. I need your feet to go where I am called. You are the answer to the people's prayers, and we go together when and where they call. I don't need your knowledge, your talent, nor your virtues. I only care about your love. Listen to the love speaking in your heart. Put love in everything you do, and I will give you the wisdom you need to be victorious.

You think you are not worthy, you think you are not enough, you think you are not loved, and yet here I stand, the Creator of the Universe, knocking at the door of your heart, begging you to let me in. That's how worthy you are, my child. I am always with you. Open up; do not prolong your pain. I love you just the way you are. Will you trust me? Will you answer my calling?

God

He folded the piece of paper and put it back in his pocket. "The following week, I packed my books and a few clothes, gave away the rest to the poor in my neighborhood, and left for the monastery. I disappointed many people when I decided to leave my job. I lost my friends, but I couldn't live with the lie anymore. I had ignored the Truth for too many years."

4.

Charlie had overheard our conversation but didn't understand a word of Romanian. He waited patiently for his opening, then thanked the priest for allowing us to visit the church and walked outside.

"Let's go, kid," he told me. "It's getting late."

"Thank you, Father," I said and bowed my head.

When I exited the church, Charlie was already waiting for me in the car. "What was that all about?" he said. "We're late. We should have been on the road by now."

I turned on the headlights and drove down the hill through clouds of dust. The forest closed in behind us.

In my mind, I had only one thought: *Why is it so difficult for us to honor the Truth in our hearts?*

CHAPTER 3

ONE NIGHT IN TRANSYLVANIA WITH THE FATHER OF THE HUBBLE SPACE TELESCOPE

(PART 2)

We live our lives like we will never die,
and nonetheless we never live at all.

1.

I was a visiting researcher at the International Space University at the NASA Kennedy Space Center in Florida when I got to know Dr. Charles Pellerin, or Charlie. He invited me for dinner at his house one evening to share life stories and talk about the impact of the social environment on the success of leaders. Throughout his 30-year career with NASA, Charlie oversaw the launch of 12 satellites and led one of the greatest scientific projects in history: the development of the Hubble Space Telescope.

The photographs of planets and galaxies taken by Hubble are iconic. *National Geographic* called Hubble the "holy grail of space exploration." The walls of Charlie's office were covered with international awards, medals, and decorations for his pioneering work in the scientific community. For his success with Hubble, NASA *twice* awarded

Charlie their Outstanding Leadership Medal, a recognition given to only 50 people in history. Before he retired, he was also awarded the Distinguished Service Medal, which NASA describes as their highest honor, given when "the contribution is so extraordinary that other forms of recognition would be inadequate."

In short, Charlie is a NASA legend.

We remained friends. A year after we met, Charlie traveled to Romania with his wife to visit UNESCO heritage sites, and I offered to show them the country.

2.

After we left the medieval monastery, Charlie and I still had a long drive ahead of us to the hotel. We were silent awhile, until I blurted out, "What happened behind the scenes with Hubble Space Telescope?"

Charlie shook his head. "Hubble was the biggest screwup in the history of science, kid," he said. "For fifteen years while we built it, Congress asked us again and again if the telescope would work. What could we have said? That we spent almost two billion dollars and didn't know? 'Of course it will work,' we told them. Well, it didn't. We sent it into space with a flawed mirror."

"How's that possible?" I asked.

Charlie replied, "After we launched Hubble, I took a week off and went to Japan for a holiday. I was flying back from Tokyo to Washington, D.C., and had a stopover in Saint Louis. I called my office to check my messages when my boss broke the news: Hubble couldn't focus. All the images were blurry. I heard his voice but didn't believe a word. He told me to find the front page of any major newspaper and read the title. So I picked up the *St. Louis Post-Dispatch* and saw it: 'National Disaster: Hubble Launched with Flawed Mirror.'"

"So, it was a technical error?"

"What kind of people do you think worked on Hubble, kid? We had the best scientists, the best engineers, and the best managers in the world. They knew what they were doing, but despite all this, the mission failed."

"What really happened behind closed doors?" I wondered.

"The mishap with Hubble led me to one of the greatest discoveries in the history of leadership," Charlie continued. "When people come together in a group, they create an invisible social environment. Every family, classroom, friendship, team, company, and country has a specific social context. This context changes our perception and alters our behaviors. We unconsciously adapt to the social environment we're in," Charlie said.

He continued, "If you go to a bar, which is a kind of social context, you have certain behaviors. If you go to a funeral, you sense the appropriate behaviors for this social situation, and you adjust to it. If you go to your grandparents' house, you encounter a different social context and adapt accordingly. This is the power of the social environment: it drives your thoughts and behaviors. You don't have to think about it, you just adapt, and it happens automatically.

"In short, when we built Hubble, we put our brilliant people in the wrong social context. We criticized them in a rage for any mistakes they'd made. We created an environment where it wasn't safe for them to tell the truth. Managers, including me, were hostile to them, and our team members wouldn't tell us of any problems that were small enough to be ignored. They made a little error when they built the mirror, but in the environment they were in, they rationalized it away, over and over, to avoid reprisal.

"The error was smaller than the width of a strand of hair—small enough to be rationalized away, but big enough to destroy the telescope. To answer your question of exactly what happened behind closed doors: We created a social context in which people were afraid to tell and act on the truth. To remain safe, they unconsciously adapted and ignored a small technical error that ruined the satellite.

"Most people will never experience a failure as traumatic as the one we've been through with Hubble. We took the failure very personally, and it shattered many of my colleagues.

"Some months after Hubble was launched into space, I gathered my team under a very different social context. We put together a servicing mission, we sent astronauts into space, and successfully repaired the telescope. That's how Hubble became the giant success it is today—one of the greatest scientific programs in history.

"What you need to keep in mind, kid, is that the social environment in which you live and work is the hidden driver of success or failure. The social context drives your thinking, your decisions, your behaviors, and your results. It's not how smart you are; it's the context you're in. If the social environment you're in doesn't empower you to succeed, you have to change it. You cannot fight it. The social context will devour your mind and make you blind to what you're doing if you let it."

3.

A couple of months after the launch of the Hubble Space Telescope, another disaster demonstrated the power of the social context.

On June 10, 1990, British Airways flight 5390 took off from Birmingham early in the morning, bound for Spain.

After a routine takeoff, First Officer Alastair Atchison gave the controls over to Captain Tim Lancaster. Two minutes into the climb, Lancaster took off his shoulder straps and switched on the autopilot. The crew was preparing breakfast in the back of the plane when they heard an explosion in the cockpit. Passengers screamed in terror as the plane shuddered and plunged toward the ground. They thought a bomb had exploded on board.

Flight attendants ran across the plane to find the cockpit filled with white fog. The captain's window had blown out at more than 17,000 feet altitude, disappearing like a bullet shot into the sky. Captain Lancaster was ripped from his seat; the wind smashed his body outside the fuselage, while his legs remained trapped inside between the seat belt and the flight controls. His knees jammed the controls forward, disconnecting the autopilot and pushing the plane into a steep dive.

They were flying into one of the busiest airspaces in the world and were now facing a midair collision with another aircraft.

Atchison fought alone to control the damaged airplane. He was shouting in his headset, but he couldn't hear the replies from Air Traffic Control. The ground controller later admitted that when he heard Atchison over the radio, he couldn't believe what he was hearing: "These things don't happen," he said in an interview for *National Geographic*. "It's something you see in movies, but they just don't happen in real life."

Flight attendant Nigel Ogden latched on to the captain's belt and legs, attempting to keep his body from being dragged farther out of the cockpit and into the engine. The hurricane in the passenger cabin flung papers and loose debris toward the cockpit. Two other crew members stepped forward to grab on to the captain's legs and relieve the exhausted, frostbitten, and bruised attendant. From the flight deck, they could see Lancaster's eyes were open, but he wasn't blinking. His poor head was battered against the fuselage. Atchison ordered the crew to hold on to the captain's body, even though they believed he was dead.

Pilot-training procedures are performed with two pilots. One is flying the plane, and the other one is doing the emergency operations. In this Hollywood-like scenario, the captain was crushed outside the fuselage, and the copilot was struggling to control the damaged aircraft and land at an airport he'd never flown into before. With 81 terrified passengers on board, Atchison made an emergency landing in Southampton Airport. Miraculously, Captain Lancaster survived. He regained consciousness in the ambulance on the way to the hospital.

When the plane stopped at the end of the runway, investigators were already there to take the case. They discovered that the aircraft had been serviced a few hours before takeoff, and the engineer on duty had replaced the old windshield with a new one. During the official questioning, he was very open about his procedure. He went into the hangar, removed the old bolts, chose the new bolts by visually measuring them against the old ones, and then put the new windshield on the plane.

According to aviation laws, engineers must check the parts catalogue and verify that the serial number on the bolts matches the serial number in the catalogue for that specific airplane. They are never supposed to decide visually, and in this case, the engineer's eyes had failed him. Some of the bolts he'd selected were a few millimeters thinner than the bolts meant for this aircraft; others were too short. When the plane ascended, the bolts didn't hold, and the pressure in the cabin blew the window out into the sky.

Stuart Culling, senior investigator with the Air Accidents Investigation Branch, hired a behavioral psychologist when he interviewed the engineer on duty. He wanted to know why an engineer who'd been with the company for two decades ignored procedures, bypassed the technical manual, and dismissed the advice of his supervisor to check the parts catalogue before replacing the bolts.

In an interview for *National Geographic*, Culling said he was horrified to hear the engineer acknowledging that he had been devising these shortcuts for years. The team had more work than they could possibly handle, and they invented strategies to finish on time. Furthermore, Culling was puzzled by the casual manner in which the engineer described his actions. It was such a serious accident, yet nobody tried to hide anything or make excuses. Culling then understood the severity of the problem: the engineer hadn't even been aware that he *was* breaking the basic safety rules. The social context he was working in influenced him to take shortcuts so often and for such a long period of time, he'd become blind to the danger of what he was doing.

4.

In the 1950s, Dr. Solomon Asch, a Polish psychologist living in New York, performed a series of experiments to study the effects of the social environment on our thinking.

In one of his studies, subjects were shown two cards. On the first card was a single line. On the second card were three lines, one of them being the same length as the line on the first card.

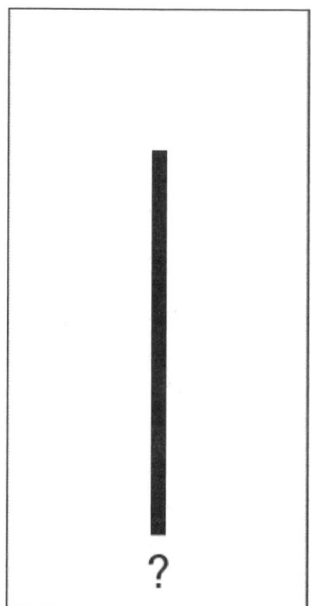 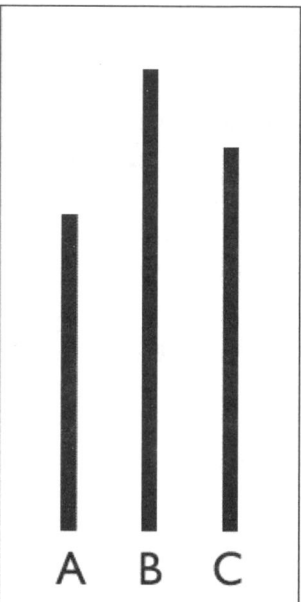

People were asked to tell which line on the second card was the same length as the line on the first card. It was an easy task, something that most children could answer correctly. All the subjects gave the right answer.

Then Asch added a twist to the experiment. The subjects were placed in a room with members of the researcher's team. These actors would examine the cards before the subjects, and then intentionally gave the wrong answer. Their conversations and behaviors created a social environment to which the subjects adapted. In this context, three out of four subjects would give *the same wrong answer* as the actors before them.

Asch passed away in 1996 and left unanswered probably the most important question of the study: Did the subjects who gave the wrong answer simply conform to the social pressure to fit in, or did the social context actually *alter their perception of reality* to the point where they weren't even aware of their error?

In 2005 Dr. Gregory Berns, a psychiatrist and neuroscientist at Emory University in Atlanta, led a similar study using advanced brain imaging technologies to find out the answer to this question. He used functional MRI scanners to observe which regions of the brain were active when people performed various mental activities. The study involved 32 volunteers who were shown objects on the computer screen and were then asked to determine if the objects were similar or different.

Before the experiment began, subjects met other people in the waiting room who they believed were also volunteers. They were, in fact, researchers, ready with fake answers. As planned, the actors gave the wrong answers in advance, and then the subjects entered the MRIs, where the brain scanner recorded the decision-making process.

Similar to Asch's experiment, 41 percent of subjects gave the wrong answer, prompted by the actors. Nothing new. Then scientists discovered something very interesting. If subjects gave the wrong answer to conform with the social pressure, they should have had increased activity in the frontal part of the brain in areas dealing with conscious decision, conflict management, and high-level mental activities. However, there was no activity in the frontal part of the brain in areas responsible for conscious thought. In fact, people who gave the wrong answer had increased activity in the brain areas dedicated to vision and spatial perception.

Simply stated, the brain turned what the social environment was showing into a decision; subjects believed they *were* deciding. People had no control over their thoughts and decisions—they just unconsciously conformed to what they were seeing in their surroundings.

On the other hand, people who gave the correct answer and opposed the judgment of the group had increased activity in brain areas dedicated to emotions of pain, fear, rejection, and excitement. Living in truth against the social environment comes with an emotional cost and various degrees of suffering.

5.

"Hubble was not NASA's most tragic failure, kid. When we don't learn our lessons, the past tends to repeat itself," continued Charlie. "A few years before we launched Hubble, I parked my car at NASA headquarters and found my team waiting at the elevator. This had never happened before.

"It was January 28, 1986. They were there to tell me that the space shuttle *Challenger* had just exploded and killed all seven astronauts on board."

NASA had launched the space shuttle *Challenger* on a frigid morning, when temperatures dropped below what the rocket had been designed for. The initial report of the investigation committee stated that the disaster happened because engineers did not understand how technology worked in low temperatures.

To Diane Vaughan, professor of sociology at Columbia University and member of the failure investigation board, this conclusion didn't make sense. How was it possible that some of the best engineers in the world did not understand technology after 24 successful flights? *Challenger* was the 25th flight of the shuttle.

Following investigations revealed that engineers did actually understand technology very well. They'd even warned managers about the danger of explosion.

Engineers made desperate attempts the night before to stop the launch, and some refused to sign the flight documents. So the real question was why did NASA managers launch the space shuttle when all evidence suggested they should not?

In the 1980s, the space shuttle was the national space transportation system for the United States. Everything going to space was flying on the space shuttle. Therefore, delaying one launch would have delayed all subsequent launches. NASA managers were under enormous pressure to keep all flights within schedule. John Young, chief astronaut at NASA and one of the very few people who walked on the moon and drove the lunar rover on its surface, said there is only one reason why a dangerous machine would be allowed to fly: launch schedule pressure.

6.

What we perceive to be the main thing in our life—in our social environment—affects how we see reality and how we make decisions. The British Airways engineer saw what the social context of the company showed him: the take-off program. NASA managers saw what the social context showed them: the launch program. In both cases, schedule became more salient than safety. Schedule became the main thing. Whether we're conscious of it or not, it doesn't matter: what we believe to be the main thing always drives our thinking, decisions, and behaviors.

"What happened to the NASA launch team as well as the British Airways engineer is now known as *normalization of deviance*, a fancy term for incremental stupidity," continued Charlie. "Diane Vaughan named it 'incremental descent into poor judgment.' In some social environments, people grow accustomed, and eventually blind, to aberrant behaviors that in the end destroy them.

"The process that allows this mental pattern to form is very simple: we take a shortcut one time, two times, three times, and then it begins to look like the normal way of doing things. In our mind, the risk factor diminishes every time we find ourselves unscathed at the end of this path, but the danger is always there, growing in the darkness of our unawareness. We do it one time, two times, three times, and it becomes a habit. Then tragedy strikes."

Our car meandered through the hills of Transylvania, and Charlie closed his eyes to rest for a few minutes. *Have I seen normalization of deviance in my life?* I wondered. Examples began showing up in my mind.

Lack of exercise is a deviant behavior that has become normal for most of us. Alcohol and drug abuse are devastating deviant behaviors that have become normal for many people. Destroying the environment for profit is a deviant behavior that has become normal. We get a sense that what we're doing is wrong, but we don't change because our actions don't hurt us in the moment.

Nobody believes a tragedy is coming. Drinking for a day, for a week, for a month, or for a year has no immediate effects. Pleasure is now; pain is in the future. Overeating and poisoning your body with bad food for a day, for a week, for a month, or for a year doesn't have tragic effects now. Stupid behaviors bring ease in the moment but come with a devastating price in the end. We keep doing what we do until it blows up in our face. A heart attack. An overdose. A disease. A broken family. A suicide. A shooting in a school. A plane crash. We suffer our way into wisdom. We fall into unawareness and realize it only when something hits us hard and wakes us up.

But by far the most tragic and deviant behavior of all is that we live our lives like we will never die, and nonetheless we never live at all. We exist, yet we never truly live. We give away too many years of our lives on work we know doesn't matter. We stay in false relationships and shadow jobs that give us as much safety as a prison cell can offer. We think and choose and do what the social environment is showing us, and we just live what we see other people doing. We suppress the love in our hearts and compromise and act against the Truth for days and months and years until we become numb to our pain, and blind to what we're doing to ourselves. We ignore our dreams and live comfortable lies that cripple our spirit, but we don't make the change to step into our destiny. This is what deviant behaviors do—bring comfort in the moment and terrible pain in the end. And one day, a phone call from the doctor gives us the wake-up call, but then it is too late.

Before we'd left the monastery, I'd prayed to understand why it is so hard for most of us to live in Truth. The conversation that followed with Charlie indirectly led me to discover the answer: The mind is a focusing and decision-making mechanism. We can focus on our spirit and decide to honor the voice of Truth, thus becoming free in the hands of God. Or, we can focus on the world and decide to take the path of least resistance, thus becoming puppets in the hands of others. There is no other choice. Both come with a price, but the first brings life and the other brings death.

A year later, I would truly learn this lesson.

CHAPTER 4

THE TRAGIC STORY OF "WHO YOU REALLY ARE"

The wise man will be nourished by the Truth.

November 2014. Bucharest.

1.

On a crisp autumn evening, I stepped outside the Masonic temple into a pitch-black parking lot. Through the curtain of rain, I made out the shape of my friend Daniel's car in the distance. Several shadows ran in all directions, holding newspapers over their heads. Their shoes drummed fast rhythms on the pavement as they hurried to get out of the rain. The last days of November had always been my favorite, bringing back the thrill of my first years of school. They are the bridge between the seasons, the moments when summer loves turn into memories, and fallen leaves turn into snow.

"Let's walk to the car. I will drive you home," said Daniel. He grabbed my arm with one hand and clutched his violin case with the other. We were both dressed in the black suit, white shirt, and dark tie required at Masonic rituals.

"We're both artists," he said. "We need to make our souls happy, even if that means ruining a good suit." He laughed as we slipped into the car and settled into our seats. "Forty years ago, when I was in college, I would take my girlfriend up on the roof of the conservatory on nights like this, and we'd make love in the rain. We didn't care if people in the street saw us. Most of them walked while looking down at puddles, their heads covered by umbrellas. We only had to make sure nobody from the university caught us. Now it is more difficult to do that, with my two patches of white hair waving above my ears like Buddhist prayer flags. Since I've turned sixty, my body has been shrinking daily. Every single part of it!" Our laughter filled the car.

Daniel had taken me under his wing at the Masonic lodge since the day I walked in as an apprentice, one year before. We met once a month at the temple, but it was enough for us to bond, to open our hearts to each other. His blue eyes held the peace of an artist, and he spoke with the kindness of an old soul.

We drove through the narrow streets of Bucharest. Daniel slowed down so as not to splatter the people on the sidewalks. From both sides of the road, the concrete apartment buildings were closing in on us. The only sounds were the classical piano music coming from the radio and the monotonous thumping of rain on the car.

"People look sad . . ." I said, looking out the window.

"What do you mean?" Daniel asked me. "What people?"

"Everyone," I said. "Nobody smiles. Everyone looks sad."

"They are truly beautiful people. What you see on their faces is the consequence of the social environment we've lived in for years. The Communist regime ended almost three decades ago and much has changed since, but the shadow of past hurts lingers still in the back of our minds," replied Daniel. "You see only their faces, but I've known many of their hearts throughout my life. Their hurt goes much deeper than a lost smile. The pain cut so deep that most of us don't feel it anymore. Hurt became normal, and a part of who we are."

I looked at him from the passenger's seat without saying a word. He gazed ahead at the road.

"Let me tell you a story," he continued. "When I was your age, the context was different from today. When you graduated from college, the Communist government gave you an apartment and a job somewhere in the country, but in exchange, they took your freedom. You had no other choice. You couldn't leave. You had to go.

"Today they don't give you an apartment or a job, but you are free. We had no freedom. We lived in a society where we couldn't express ourselves. They threw you in prison if you said the wrong thing in public, or even from the privacy of your home, if they found out. Your parents, along with millions of others, lived in a social environment ruled with fear. Their smallest yearning to be free, to be themselves, was punished. They had to adapt in order to survive. They put their hearts in solitary confinement for years and forgot about it." Daniel paused for a while to let that sink in.

"If you were to live in a social structure that punished you for speaking and living the Truth, do you think you'd suppress yourself and shut up about who you are? Would you do what is safe, rather than what is true?"

I pressed my forehead against the cold glass window of the car, and stared at the raindrops trickling down. I could see my eyes reflected in the glass whenever we passed a light pole.

"When you deny and block the Truth in your heart, when you don't express your love and don't live who you truly are, fear invades the mind and pain invades the body. You become desperate to cope with the pain, and the closest balm at hand is usually the bottle," said Daniel. "Of my thirty-five classmates in high school, all except two drank themselves to death."

I stared at the shadows walking on the sidewalk, and the pools our car whooshed through. Faces of my friends and relatives flashed in my mind.

"What we don't bring into light, and don't acknowledge to ourselves, grows in the dark," continued Daniel. "Jesus told us in the Gospel of Thomas that if we bring forth what is within us, what we bring forth will save us. If we do not bring forth what is within us, what we do not bring forth will destroy us. In the environment I grew up in, people blocked their heart's will and ignored the Truth in order to survive."

2.

Alcohol or drug dependence is oftentimes a consequence of not being able to cope with your social context—not being able to bear being present in your own life. One of the fundamental causes of addiction was discovered by Dr. Bruce Alexander, professor emeritus in psychology, who performed the following experiment in the 1970s.

Dr. Alexander's team built two different types of settings for rats. The rats in the standard laboratory cages were isolated. They couldn't see or touch other rats, and they had nothing to do. In the large, enriched environment known as "Rat Park," the rats had good food, running wheels for exercise, toys for mental stimulation, platforms for climbing, tin cans for hiding, and many other rats to socialize with.

In both environments, the rats had access to two drinking bottles: a bottle of water and a bottle of water with morphine in it, an opiate very similar to heroin. At the end of each day, researchers measured the two bottles to see if rats preferred the pure water or the morphine water. The rats in solitary confinement almost always chose the morphine water. They always became addicted, with many drinking themselves to death. In Rat Park, they almost never drank morphine water, preferring instead to socialize and play with one another.

Rats are social, sexual, and working beings, just like humans. People who become addicted don't have to be put in cages, wrote Professor Alexander. It's enough for people only to *feel* caged—in a job, in a classroom, in a relationship, in a family, or in a country—and they will drink or take drugs to cope with the situation. Professor Alexander suggested that addiction is an escape from a social environment where human connection—with yourself and with others—is impossible.

In another experiment, Alexander forced isolated rats to drink only morphine water for 57 days. If our cultural story about addiction were true—that chemicals in drugs take over our brain—then two months of drinking morphine should have been enough to create addiction. However, when the "addicted" rats were moved to Rat Park, they stopped drinking the morphine water. They chose the pure water instead. After a period of withdrawal, they adapted to the happy environment and changed their behavior.

While Professor Alexander was studying the effects of the social environment on rats, the Vietnam War was wreaking havoc on the other side of the world. According to a study published in the *Archives of General Psychiatry*,

20 percent of the American soldiers fighting in Vietnam were addicted to heroin. The public and the media in the United States were terrified that hundreds of thousands of veterans would come back as junkies. But this never happened. Instead, the soldiers returned home, and 95 percent of those who were addicted stopped using heroin within one year.

In his book *Chasing the Scream*, Johann Hari wrote that those rats in Alexander's experiments and the soldiers in Vietnam weren't victims of the drug, but of their *environments*. Addiction was their way of coping with "being dislocated from everything that gave them meaning," wrote Hari. When you feel caged and your world becomes intolerable, you leave—physically if you can, mentally if you cannot. When soldiers changed their environment, they changed their behavior. They returned home to a meaningful life, and they gave up the drugs.

It makes sense that people who live in a social context where they are able to connect with others and bond with their work are much less likely to become addicted, even if they have alcohol and drugs all around. After all, they want to be present in their own lives. But if they feel trapped or caged in a situation, a job, or a relationship, if they cannot bond because they live in a social environment that punishes them for expressing who they are, they will find refuge in whatever takes the pain away.

Professor Peter Cohen, director of the Centre for Drug Research at the University of Amsterdam, wrote that we have a fundamental human need to bond with our work and with others. We can bond only if we open our hearts to the Truth in our lives, in our relationships with ourselves and with others. Relationships (e.g., with people, with our work, with God) are either full and complete, or they are not at all. There is no in-between. People bond when they are authentic, open, and honest, or they do not bond at all.

We've all been through friendships, romantic relationships, or work or family relations in which we knew that we were not authentic and too uncomfortable to be sincere. If we don't acknowledge the truth in our relationships, they simply become a state of isolation with somebody (some body) still around. Staying miserable in a meaningless job for too long puts our heart in an unbearable cage. The pain becomes depression if turned inward, and anger if turned outward. Addiction is only a hopeless attempt to deal with the pain of living cut off from who we really are.

As Professor Alexander said in a lecture in London in 2011, "Human beings only become addicted . . . when they desperately need to fill the emptiness that threatens to destroy them. The need to fill an inner void is not limited to people who become drug addicts, but afflicts the vast majority of people."

3.

"If you deny, ignore, repress, or rationalize away the Truth long-term, it will shatter you." Daniel punctuated each word with a slap on the steering wheel with the palm of his hand.

"Times have changed, and people are free today," I said. "It's different."

"Don't be naive," he said. "You don't need to live in a social context like Communism to feel caged and not able to find meaning in life. Your own mind, your unconscious beliefs, a toxic friendship or family relationship can choke your freedom to express who you are, with the same tragic effects. Your heart's calling—your will—is only love and cannot be anything else. Do you always live, act, and express your love? Do you feel free? Let me tell you a story . . .

"My grandfather used to tell me that Mother Nature has infinite wisdom, and if you are patient, she will reveal her mysteries. Many years ago, as I was walking with him in the garden, he asked me to water the flowers. I took the hose and ran my fingers through the rushing water, while my grandpa told me this parable:

> 'Danny, in this world, you are very much like a water hose in the garden. Love flows through you, just as water runs through this hose. Love comes from God, just as water comes from the well. The water doesn't depend on the hose, just as God doesn't depend on you. But the water needs the hose to pour on the garden, and the flowers need the water. God needs you to pour his love in the world, and people need his love.
>
> 'Your mind is your thumb. When you use your thumb to partially cover the flow, the pressure increases. The more you block the flow, the greater the pressure. If you cover the hose completely, it is only a matter of time before it blows up.
>
> 'When you cover or suppress the calling of God in your heart, when you think and act opposite to Truth, you block the flow of love through you—and pressure builds up. If you do this for years, it blows up: anger if expressed outward, depression if expressed inward. Then, it is only a matter of time before your body falls ill.
>
> 'Just as the water continues to push through the hose when your fingers block the flow, love continues to flow through you when your mind blocks its expression. All you must do is remove the blocks in your mind and

express yourself in love. Set love free, and you become free. Ancient spiritual teachers spoke the truth when they said our task is not to find love, but merely to remove all blocks we have built against it.'

"Your will flows through your heart, and pulls you toward what you truly value in life. When you embrace it, you find meaning. When you block it, you find pain. You can choose one or the other—but you can't have both. Love is the force that pulls you to follow your dreams, to reveal and express yourself, to explore, to discover, to create, and to bond. Whenever your behaviors conflict with your will, whenever you think and act against Truth, tension grows within yourself. Strain turns into pain. Anger, anxiety, and depression follow with certainty, as darkness follows the sunset. This is why Jesus said that the kingdom divided against itself will be destroyed, and the house divided against itself will fall (Mark 3:24–25). Mind against heart, and behavior against will—it will break you."

"Thus the mind becomes a prison," I mused.

Daniel went on. "There's a profound wisdom in the words of Jesus: 'The spirit indeed is willing, but the flesh is weak' (Matthew 26:41). I have a friend who is project manager for a financial corporation, but her dream is to open a restaurant. Her spirit is willing to start this new business. Every time she thinks about her calling, her heart fills with enthusiasm. She feels love flowing through her. But in an instant, her mind drags her in the opposite direction: *What if it doesn't work? I am in my thirties, and I have a child. What will my parents say about me quitting my job after they supported me through college?* She doesn't want to, but she then acts as she thinks she should, and stays in her job without the true will to do so.

"Everyone envies her. She earns a great paycheck, has a loving husband and a beautiful child, but she's sinking into depression. She feels even worse when she looks around her because she has no apparent reason to feel depressed. The truth is she has the *only* reason to feel depressed: her heart is screaming from a golden cage, and she doesn't listen. The greater the gap between what love *calls* you to do and what you *actually* do, the deeper the depression you can fall into.

"The way to find joy is to leave the cage, not to decorate it and make it prettier. Why do you think the waiting rooms of psychologists and psychiatrists are filled with successful people who realized after twenty or thirty years of work that money, a career, a house in the suburbs do not bring peace of mind and joy of heart? They keep hoping that by changing the external conditions of their lives—earn more money, be in better physical shape, have another partner, or travel more—it will change how they feel. It never works because the emptiness is not around them. The emptiness is *within* them. The only way to come back to life is to acknowledge and follow the voice arising from your heart, calling you to return to love, to return to Truth.

"An old proverb states that if you follow your heart in life, you will not have regrets. You will be defeated, you will suffer, but you will not have regrets. All of us are familiar with the pain and suffering of having a dream and not knowing how to make it a reality. But pain and suffering are not the same. They are opposite to each other.

"Pain shows up every time you deny, ignore, or rationalize away the Truth: You want to work with children, but you don't. You want to become a writer, but you don't. You want to start your own business, but you don't. What your heart calls you to do, but you don't, creates pain. Pain is unbearable because Truth is denied, and lies are made real in your mind. Excuses create pain because you are not using your mind to think how you can fulfill your will, but rather to make real the reasons why your love should be ignored and Truth rejected. Pain leads to anxiety, anger, and depression, which in turn lead to drinking, drug abuse, or violence. These are desperate attempts to take your pain away, but they never work because Truth cannot be denied and the flow of love cannot be blocked. When you begin lying to yourself about who you are, when you repress your dreams and ignore what is important to you, when the mask becomes the person and the person forgets the person and becomes the mask, you become your own worst enemy. You are attacking yourself from within, and there's nobody there to protect you. Your life becomes a shadow drama, and you become a crippled version of yourself.

"We all have a natural gift, a dream that calls us to return to love. Very few actually have the circumstances and the social environment to nurture that gift. We have to make them. We *must* make them. When you deny or ignore the Truth, in your heart you know you are hiding. You know what you value, and you know what you care about the most. It may be a little thing, but it means the world to you. You also know that you have turned away from your heart. You are angry because you feel caged in a job or a relationship you don't want to be in. You blame your circumstances, but you are actually angry with yourself for your incapacity to rip off the bandage and the bondage, and walk out into freedom. You raise your hand to the sky while holding the key to freedom in the other, but not daring to open the door and run. The longer you live a comfortable lie, the farther you drift from your purpose, and the harder it will be to gather the courage to go back to your heart.

"When you embrace the Truth, pain goes away in an instant. Truth gives you life and makes you free when you act on it. Your life has meaning and your mind, your heart, and your actions are aligned. You stand in power. As Jesus said in the Book of Thomas the Contender: 'The wise man will be nourished by the Truth.' Suffering will show up and trials will come, but they will be nothing more than minor setbacks and small knocks that you'll get along the way. At the end of the journey, pain will bring regret, but suffering will bring joy.

"Suffering is practicing my violin until my fingers bleed. Pain is taking the violin away from me. Suffering is getting hurt in the game. Pain is being on the sidelines. Suffering is reading the rejection letters for your manuscript. Pain is never daring to write or send in the work. Suffering is customers not wanting your product. Pain is you never building your product. Suffering is people not caring about your work. Pain is you not caring about you work. Suffering comes in a battle that has meaning to you, and is worth fighting. Pain comes by turning away from what is meaningful to you.

"Viktor Frankl once wrote in *Man's Search for Meaning*, 'Man's main concern is not to gain pleasure or to avoid pain but rather to see a meaning in his life. That is why man is even ready to suffer, on the condition, to be sure, that his suffering has a meaning.' The only way to be free and find meaning is to live in Truth, even if you have to rise against the immediate social structures. Truth cannot be blocked, ignored, or rationalized away."

We drove for a few minutes in silence, and Daniel turned the radio up a little louder to listen to his favorite piano piece. I stared into the night, through the pouring rain.

There are people who, even today, live in extreme circumstances, I thought. *But most of us, the great majority of us, what excuse do we have not to live in Truth and follow our dreams? What excuse do I have? There is none . . .*

CHAPTER 5

IT AIN'T EASY TO BE FRANK

We justify the pain that grows inside of us
for a reason we are not even aware of.

May 2015. The Arizona Desert.

1.

The lower crescent of the moon glimmered above the Arizona desert, and the first star of the night winked on the opposite side of the sky. The red rocks on the horizon turned purple in the dusk. I walked across a wooden pathway, trying to find my way to a dark house. There was to be a Native American gathering, but the friend who invited me had just called to tell me that he would not be attending tonight.

My shadow lagged behind me in the light of oil lamps that flickered at knee level. Birds became silent in the twilight, and a wind chime rustled in the garden, longing for the tree it once had been a part of. Two horses grazed close to the wire fence. In the distance, a few coyotes grieved the coming of the night.

"You must be Dragos," a voice called. A woman rushed out of the house in front of me, carrying two paper platters. "Follow me into the backyard—everybody's there."

A man with a thick British accent kissed my cheeks, then introduced me to the handful of people sitting around the camping table. One by one, their faces were illuminated by the light bulb hanging from a wire above them: Albert, the Englishman, in his 50s; a hippie couple in their 30s from California; and Aiyana, the woman who showed me the way.

Aiyana was a Native American woman in her 20s. She had coal-black eyes and straight raven hair that flowed over her bare back. The black shawl across her shoulders swooped to reveal the tattoo of a barbed-wire dream catcher with a wolf paw in the center and two eagle feathers underneath.

A guy with a straw cowboy hat sat by himself behind us on an empty wooden beer box, playing acoustic guitar. The others asked him to play one of his songs three times in a row, and even the coyotes in the desert remained quiet as he strummed. His red shirt was unbuttoned, showing a well-built body and three silver dog tags hanging from his neck. He raised his eyes from his guitar only to tell me his name, Frank, and to politely decline when others passed him a beer or invited him to join the table. He continued to play his guitar but didn't sing a word.

Aiyana paused to kiss and caress Frank's cheeks on her way to the kitchen. Between songs, he patted the rottweiler sleeping on his boots. The corners of his mouth lifted when people gave him a round of applause, but his eyes never smiled.

2.

After dinner, I joined Albert and Aiyana in the kitchen, while the rest stayed outside to prepare for the drumming ceremony. Albert and I were in foam to our elbows, and Aiyana was standing next to us, drying the dishes.

"You see those dog tags he wears?" Although Albert was speaking to me, his eyes looked through the window at Frank. "They belonged to his two best friends. They both died in Iraq. They went there together, but only Frankie came home."

"He's very quiet," I said.

"He just turned twenty-five," said Aiyana. "He went to war after he finished high school and just came back last year."

"He's a wonderful kid," said Albert. "He went to school in Texas; he was a musician and played in the church band. They toured the world with their concerts. They played throughout Asia, Europe, and Africa, and all over America. Not many kids have the chance to see the world before they turn eighteen. He had the kindest heart in the world, talent that other musicians would sell their souls for, and a great future ahead of him."

Aiyana was silent. Her lips trembled, and her eyes welled up with tears. She turned her head away from us.

"Frank was raised in a very religious family," Albert continued. "His heart had always been with music, but his parents pushed him to become a minister. He was only a teenager, but according to their rules, he had to have a family at eighteen and serve his country. So he got married when he finished high school and joined the Army."

"They sent him to Iraq," Aiyana explained, tears now falling down her cheeks.

"He was a machine-gun operator," said Albert. "Frankie. This innocent child! They put him on top of a tank with a machine gun in his hand. For six damned years."

"What's he doing now?" I asked.

"Frank stopped here for a few weeks to help me rebuild my roof," said Albert. "He came to my property as a 'WWOOFer.' That's what they call people who join up with the Worldwide Opportunities on Organic Farms. They'll usually spend half a day helping out on the property, receiving free accommodation and meals in return. Lots of young people see it as a great opportunity to travel the world on little money. Aiyana is also WWOOFing on the farm. She's been here for three months."

"Frank is driving across the country with Gracie, the dog you see at his feet," said Aiyana. "I'm in love with him and would gladly join his travels, but he wants to be alone."

"He lost everything. The Army took even his soul away," said Albert. "When he returned home last year, his closest friends were dead. His wife divorced him while he was away. He moved to San Francisco for a while. He didn't want to go back to Texas. He spent half a year alone in his apartment."

"It's a miracle he's with us today," said Aiyana.

"What do you mean?" I asked.

"I planned to kill myself." Frank suddenly appeared at the kitchen door. Albert's eyes filled with tears when he saw him standing there. Frank continued. "I had been alone for many months, and last year I decided to kill myself on Christmas Day. A few days before Christmas, though, I met an ex-Marine walking his dog on my street. He told me about this shelter where I could go and take a dog home. He said the pup helped him deal with his depression.

"I thought about it for a couple of days, but I didn't see the point. Why take a dog home if I'm just going to die soon? Well, Christmas Eve came, and I decided to go anyway to see what's with this shelter. When I walked in, the lady at the front told me they didn't have any adoptable dogs—just this rottweiler that nobody wants because people are afraid of her—and that I should come back after the holidays. She didn't know that day was supposed to be my last day alive."

Gracie walked into the kitchen, wagging her tail. She rubbed her head on Frank's jeans while he stroked her.

"I took her and planned to keep her for three days, then bring her back to the shelter," said Frank. "Three days turned into a week. We spent Christmas and New Year's together. I took her for a drive along the Pacific coast, and we roamed the city together. She messed up my plans, so here we are half a year later." Frank took out his phone and showed us a picture of him and Gracie, both wearing Santa hats, in front of a Christmas tree. "She saved my life."

"He needs time to heal," said Albert. "These kids who've gone to war need time to heal. They are good people with beautiful hearts that ended up in the wrong bloody environment." Albert turned off the tap, wiped his hands on a towel, and looked straight at me. "Did you know that more soldiers lose their lives by committing suicide than dying in battle?"

Albert walked across the room and pulled a thick tome from his bookcase. "Look," he said, flipping through pages of newspaper clippings and scientific studies. Headlines and article snippets caught my eye: *The Guardian*, February 1, 2013, "U.S. Military Struggling to Stop Suicide Epidemic among War Veterans": "More of America's serving soldiers died at their own hands than in pursuit of the enemy . . ." *The New York Times*, May 15, 2013, "Baffling Rise in Suicides Plagues the U.S. Military." *TIME*, January 10, 2014, "Report: Suicide Rate Soars among Young Vets":

"The number of male veterans under 30 ending their own lives jumps by 44 percent in two years . . ."

"Nobody has a clue why this is happening, or how to stop these young people from turning into another statistic," said Albert. "If you tell them, they won't listen because they think they know better. But science has removed from the equation the only parameter that can actually save them. Researchers look at all the details that could be the cause of this problem—depression, drug abuse, medication, early or less-than-honorable discharge, a failed relationship back home—but they cannot agree, because it doesn't make sense. We've all lost our jobs, had failed businesses, broke up with our girlfriends, and suffered, but we didn't take our lives. Depression is the effect of something far greater, something that most people don't even know of. Alcohol or drug abuse are desperate attempts to alleviate the pain caused by depression. These events in our lives can, and will, become the way we justify the pain that grows inside of us for a reason we are not even aware of."

3.

Albert, Aiyana, Frank, and I gathered around the coffee table. Albert tore a piece of paper from a notebook and drew three discontinuous concentric circles. He explained as he drew, "The center is your spirit—what you really are. The spirit is only love, and is never anything else."

Aiyana remarked, "In the Native American traditions, the center is called *chante ishta*, the single eye of the heart. 'The lamp of the body is the eye,' as Jesus said (Matthew 6:22). If your eye is bright—meaning, if your heart is pure—your whole body is lighted."

"Your spirit—the mustard seed in the center of your heart—has no polarity and no opposite," Albert continued. "All your spirit wants is to express itself, through love, as love. This is the divine will, flowing through you as you, and it is the only power that will fill your heart. Nothing else will." He drew lines coming out of the center circle. "The rays that shine from the center represent your will and your love: the Truth. The power that flows outward from your heart is only love. This is what you really are. Do you understand?" Albert tapped the center of the drawing several times, then paused.

"Yes," we said, gathering closer to look at the drawing.

"Your mind, however, can block your spirit from expressing itself," Albert said, running his finger along the outer two circles, upon which he wrote *conscious mind* and *subconscious mind*.

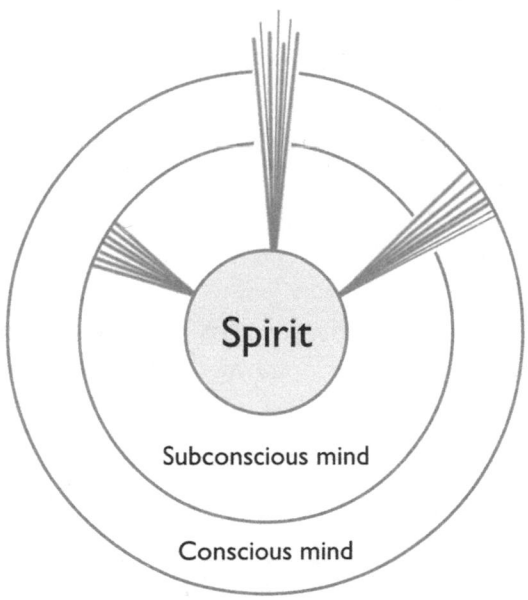

Albert continued, "Frankie, for example, your heart's calling is music. It is your love, and your enthusiasm. When you played with the band, your spirit expressed itself in the world by sharing what you loved—your music.

"A conscious blockage at one moment was: 'I don't have money to buy a guitar.' We all have these blocks. You accepted this blockage, but you didn't become a prisoner of it because you knew it was only temporary, and so you worked to find a solution. You set your music aside for a few months, you got a job to get the resources you needed to buy the instrument, and then you returned to your passion.

"The subconscious blockages are dangerous because they are built in time. We are not always aware of them, and they are usually driven by the environment we grew up in. Because we look from within, through the filters of our minds, outward, we see these blockages as reality, but they are nothing more than stories we tell ourselves. Stories like: 'I need to do what my family wants me to or they will never love me.' People can live with the false belief that they are not enough all their lives.

"Frankie, in your case your subconscious blocks were built by your family, and by your teachers in your little town: 'You must become a minister,' 'You must get married,' and 'You must serve your country.' If these beliefs had been aligned with love's calling, they would have been your greatest assets, but they opposed the Truth, and you acted against your will for years. When your subconscious beliefs block your spirit from expressing itself, this eventually destroys you."

We were all silent, looking at one another.

"Do you remember when Jesus told people that unless we change and become like little children, we cannot enter the kingdom of heaven?" Albert asked, pointing to the sketch. "When children are born, only their subconscious mind is active; it comes pure, without any blockages. Their spirit flows free. The conscious mind develops later. If you look at a baby, you see God's love pouring through her eyes. There's nothing in her mind to block it. The kingdom of heaven is not outside, somewhere. The kingdom of heaven is within us, and we find it by looking deeper and deeper inward. We discover God in our life when we become like children, and remove all the conscious and subconscious barriers we have raised to block the expression of love.

"Underneath your conscious and unconscious beliefs, love continues to flow, willing to extend outward, and express yourself. The ultimate purpose of your spirit—which is what you really are—is freedom. The spirit can and will get rid of the body if you cannot flow free, because dark beliefs cannot block God's will—which is the full expression of love—for too long a period of time. We call this *illness*.

"We have been trained to ignore our love and suppress the Truth. In the military, the Truth in our hearts is silenced with a shout: 'That's an order, Soldier!' We have been doing this for so long that these kids cannot even tell right from wrong. All of us are responsible for their lives. They are trapped in a terrible context, between the hammer and the anvil, between the cry from the inside if they kill against their will and the draconian punishments from the outside if they don't. If you think this is nonsense, look at statistics. Do you think the situation is getting worse because we are doing the right thing?

"Stanley Prusiner, M.D., said in an interview about his Nobel Prize award: 'Concepts are vindicated by the constant accrual of data and independent verification of data. No prize, not even a Nobel Prize, can make something true that is not true.' The consequences speak for themselves.

"Carl Sagan once said: 'The truth may be puzzling. It may take some work to grapple with. It may be counterintuitive. It may contradict deeply held prejudices. It may not be consonant with what we desperately want to be true. But our preferences do not determine what's true.' This reality must be acknowledged because the price we otherwise pay is devastating."

4.

Albert put his hand on his chest as he continued speaking. "Our heart's will is never to harm. The will of your heart is to hold dear, to protect, and to love. Your heart doesn't care about what you think is good or bad, right or wrong. It doesn't care about how much money you make, what the orders are, or what the law says—which is really nothing more than what other people say. Your heart cares only to express and expand by sharing love.

"However, you do have the freedom to think and act against love. The environment you are in can influence your mind and drive you to suppress your will, causing you to behave in ways you know are wrong. This will drag you into the darkest depression.

"A few years ago, the military suicide rate was much lower. Experts believed that because the military provided them with a steady income and many benefits, this helped protect the young recruits from self-harm. But a decade later, suicide rates soared. What do you think happened?" asked Albert.

We looked at one another and shrugged our shoulders.

"The war began," he said. "The context changed. The same people with the same benefits went to war, and found themselves in a different context. During times of peace, the context empowers us to embrace the Truth and honor our will, which is to protect, to help, and to serve. During war, the context forces us to march against our will. We harm instead of protecting, we destroy instead of creating, we punish instead of forgiving. Deep down, we know what we're doing is wrong, but we explain it away over and over and over until we become blind to how we hurt ourselves.

"Dr. Jonathan Woodson, assistant secretary of defense for health affairs, nailed it when he said, 'There is a difference between a military at war and a military at peace. There is no doubt that war changes you.' When good people are put in social environments that force them to think and act against love, especially when they have to kill or to be part of a system that kills, the consequence can only be pain. We cannot plant the seeds of death and reap life, scatter suffering and gather bliss!"

Albert stood, walked over to his desk, and picked up a globe of the earth. "This is what astronauts see when they fly into space," he said, spinning the globe in his palm. "All of us live here, on this spaceship Earth. We travel together through the universe on this little blue ball. Everything that happens on this planet doesn't just happen. We do it *to* each other. This is the reality, and the most simple fact. We do it to each other."

Albert put the globe back on his desk and returned to where we were sitting, again picking up his drawing with the three circles. "Our purpose in life is to live from the spirit, from the heart, from this center. We must summon the courage to think and act in ways greater than our beliefs, greater than the social circumstances, and extend only love. To be frank, it's not easy—but it's the only way. Everything we do against love and against Truth will only injure us."

Aiyana caressed Frank's face, and I gave Gracie a hug.

"That's what saved you, kid." Albert directed this at Frank but looked sweetly at Gracie. "You returned to love. You found Gracie and gave her all your love last Christmas. You found the cracks in your mind that allowed love to burst through." Albert pointed at his drawing again, at the gaps in the circles that depicted the conscious and the subconscious mind. "You gave your love to this dog, and your heart flowed through the cracks. You then returned to music. You returned to traveling. You allowed more of your true self to shine through every day that you returned to love."

Frank smiled as he put his hand around Aiyana's waist and pulled her into a warm embrace.

"One day, you will eventually love yourself enough to love Aiyana, this beautiful woman who cares for you so much," Albert said softly, looking at Frank. "You cannot feel her love for you now—not because she doesn't love you, but because you do not love yourself. She loves your light, and she loves your darkness. She loves you for who you are, kid, because you are *enough* just the way you are. God knows I love you like a son.

"With a true heart, ask God for forgiveness for anything you believe you've done wrong. Nothing is covered that will not be revealed, and everything hidden will come out to light. But what you keep hidden will torment you until you bring it out to light.

"Carl Jung, the renowned psychiatrist, said, 'The most terrifying thing is to accept oneself completely.' Do not be afraid. Tell God everything you fear to acknowledge, because he cannot heal what you conceal, and he will heal everything you reveal. Science, meditation techniques, and religious practices cannot heal you or give you peace. They deal with the conscious and the subconscious. Don't expect people, including yourself, to do only what God can do.

"Ask for forgiveness every day and be patient, no matter how long it takes. Cry as many tears as you have to cry, because sorrow brings you first to repentance, then to forgiveness, then to love, and in the end back to life. The tears of repentance wash your spirit pure. Pray until your heart doesn't condemn you anymore, because beyond the pain you are now feeling, peace awaits you.

"God loves all of us, no matter how big our errors are. You don't see it now, but keep returning to love every day. Come back again and again, with every thought you have, and in everything you do, because love never fails. And one day, when the cracks have become big enough because you have given so much love to others, you will finally get to love yourself—and maybe do so for the first time."

5.

When the clock struck midnight, the couple from California began the drumming ceremony in the backyard, by the fire. The man thudded a reindeer-skin drum with a rabbit fur beater, and the woman played her redwood flute. Albert sat down on a log and hummed the melody with his eyes closed. Frankie and Aiyana sat on a blanket in a tight embrace, holding hands. They looked peaceful, with the light of the flames reflecting in their eyes. There is a common saying that time heals all wounds. It's not true, though. Time heals nothing. *God* heals everything when we open ourselves to him, in spirit and in truth.

I walked to my car and drove in silence through the pitch-black Arizona desert. The only light came from the sky above me. The moon glowed, and the sky glimmered as if a bucket of stars had been spilled over the horizon. Suddenly, the "Pale Blue Dot," the famous image of the earth from space, flashed in my mind for a second. In this photograph of our planet taken by the Voyager-1 space probe from a distance of more than 4 billion miles away, the earth appears as a tiny dot against the dark vastness of space.

I understood in that moment what Jesus meant when he said we live in the world, but we are not *of* this world (John 17:26).

Our planet travels through the infinity of space and time, and in one moment we show up here. We call this moment our *time of birth*. We do what we do, we study, we work, we travel, we struggle, we bond, we rejoice, we suffer, and we love. Years later, in yet another moment, we leave just as we have arrived: in the arms of others, with nothing in our hands. We call this moment our *time of death*.

I don't know what lies before we come, or what awaits us after we go. What I do know is that we come through our parents, but we do not belong *to* our parents. We are the sons and daughters of the living God. We carry his spirit in our hearts, and we have only one purpose in between the two moments in time: to do the will of our Heavenly Father.

There are many voices in the world. The social environment will try to mold us in the image and likeness of man. People will influence us one way or another, but we have in our hearts the voice of God, calling us in every moment to return to love, to return to Truth. We have been given everything we need to make our dreams a reality, and fulfill our destiny. Believe it or not, the freedom to do so is ours.

LIVE YOUR DREAM

When your pockets are empty,
go where your heart is full.

— DR. DRAGOS

CHAPTER 6

YOUNG, BROKE, CRAZY, AND IN LOVE

What's this life all about?
What do I want?

2003. Bucharest.

1.

At the age of 19, I waved good-bye to my hometown and set off for college. To keep me in school, my parents put $100 in my bank account each month, which was all they could afford. Still, when I got off the train in Bucharest, I didn't have a place to rest my head at night. There was nowhere to store my luggage. Instead, I roamed the streets for a week.

Every morning, I'd carry my backpack with me, which contained a pen, some paper, a fork, a spoon, and a pillow. After classes, I walked the city with my eyes glued to the plastic hour hand of my watch until it touched 11 P.M. I'd then get on the last train of the day, which was always empty, and doze with my head on the backpack, my arms clenched tightly around it.

I'd wake up and get off at the stop before we got to the slums with ramshackle houses, gypsy florists, ticket scalpers, stray dogs, and mud roads. I'd cross the tracks and head to a friend's apartment, where I'd sleep in an armchair. Three people slept in the bed next to me.

One night, one of the women who lived in the apartment told me, "You have a week to find a place." So I adjusted my schedule. I'd tiptoe in at midnight, after she had fallen asleep, and slink out before sunrise, while she was still hitting the snooze button. Finally, my dad slipped an envelope filled with cash to the administrator of the students' dormitory, and by the end of the week I had moved into the upper bed of a bunk.

I spent my first college summer behind the counter of a music store, convincing fathers to buy kids their first guitars. This job raised my pocket money to $200 for a couple of months. Then, for almost a year, I worked as a television technician. I carried a wooden box the size of a coffin with lighting equipment and microphones. That damned box was so heavy that my right hand got longer and thinner, and my fingers turned from green to purple to black every other day.

Everywhere I roamed—from college, to work, to bars, to dates—I always showed up in blue jeans and a black T-shirt, leather bracelets on my right hand and prayer beads on my left. I played in a rock band for three years and grossed a grand total of $20 revenue from all our concerts combined. I was too shy to have one-night stands, but I did have a couple of yearlong relationships. These all ended the same way: with me running away and hiding from my girlfriends in bookstores or guitar shops.

In the last year of college, I fell in love with a sweet girl, a kindergarten teacher whom all children adored. We spent our evenings together walking hand in hand, making out on a bench in the park, talking psychology and philosophy neither of us really understood, having existential conversations, making love in my dormitory room, in the wardrobe, in the shower, in the university classrooms, and anywhere on campus where we found ourselves alone. We moved in together, and we loved each other beyond this world.

2008. Bucharest.

2.

After a five-year sentence in college in Romania, I threw my graduation cap up in the air, then promptly signed on the dotted line for another four years of a doctoral program in Germany. I was still, however, living in Romania. Every three months, I boarded a Lufthansa flight bound for Frankfurt and presented my work at the university. Then I'd head back home.

I got a job as a research assistant with the Romanian Space Agency. My days slowly took on a familiar routine. I fell out of bed around nine in the morning, elbowed my way onto a crowded subway, and read from a spiritual book on my way to work. As I got into the office, my steps raised clouds of dust from carpets that hadn't been washed since man stepped on the moon. I'd grab a plastic cup of green tea, then collapse in my chair, tired from the commute. For eight hours every day, I'd stare at my computer screen, wondering what I had gotten myself into. The scientific papers looked to me like a freeze-frame of the Brownian motion made by numbers, and Latin, and Greek letters in a boiling alphabet soup: they were everywhere and made no sense. At the end of each month, I received a check for a few hundred dollars, although the amount varied according to the mood of the politicians.

A line divided my life in two, straight through five o'clock. By day, I created prototypes for aerospace software. At sunset, you'd find me studying ancient spiritual texts under a solitary tree, and praying during the night.

Every night, before I fell asleep, I spent an hour with my hands under my head, staring at the lights and shadows moving across my ceiling. *What's this life all about?* I wondered. *What do I* want? The voice of the Universe called me to explore the end of the world, to travel to the coldest and most remote places on earth. I wanted to sail the frozen oceans, to be surrounded by glaciers, to kayak among whales and icebergs in Antarctica, to chase the aurora borealis, and trek the remote islands of the Arctic. My heart was a compass that pointed toward the North and the South Poles.

I was now 23 years old. I had never left Europe before. Polar expeditions cost as much as an apartment in Bucharest. I wasn't going to open a credit line just to travel, and then spend 15 years paying back the money. My savings account showed about $100, and my salary was enough only to take me on a train ride in Romania.

The months passed; autumn turned to winter. One Friday night, as I left the office and walked the lonely streets of Bucharest, snow began to fall. Flakes grooved like jazz dancers under the yellow street lights before landing on my face. My goatee turned white, my skin cold and wet. The snowflakes had traveled a long way from up there in heaven just to cling to my eyelashes for a moment and say hello to me. They then let go, sliding into tiny drops of water on my cheeks.

I looked up toward the sky. I pledged, "For one year, I will do whatever it takes to find a way to go to the North and the South Poles."

CHAPTER 7

GOING NORTH, GOING SOUTH

*What appealed to me was the suffering
they endured. A strange ambition burned in me
to experience those same sufferings.*

2009. Bucharest.

1.

When I opened a map of the world, my eyes dropped to the lowest point. My heart pointed *south*, but every neuron in my brain and every cell in my body pulsated with doubt. Antarctica seemed too far away. The Arctic was a lot closer to me in Romania. *I might have a chance to go north*, I thought to myself. *I will try north first.*

Nobody lives at the geographic North Pole because it is covered by ocean water and ice, constantly shifting and drifting. It's freezing in winter, melting in summer. For one month, I wrote hundreds of letters to people who might take me with them to the Arctic islands. I wrote to universities and polar research centers, to travel agencies and expedition companies, to Russian fishing boats that sailed the waters of the Arctic Ocean, and to Finnish icebreakers that crushed their way north. Nowadays, technology has opened for us the most hostile places on earth, but two centuries ago reality was very different for the first Arctic explorers.

For more than 300 years, explorers tried to traverse the Northwest Passage, which connects Europe with Asia across the top of North America, but all returned defeated. In 1845, Sir John Franklin sailed into the icebound waters of the North Pole. He left England with two ships to navigate the dark side of the Arctic. A whaling boat saw Franklin's ships on the coast of Greenland, and from there they sailed into oblivion. More than 120 men disappeared into the unknown.

Years later, Inuit elders told the story of Franklin's expedition to another British explorer who lived with them in the Arctic. They remembered meeting some *koblunas* (strangers to their land) who were dragging a boat across the island. They slogged against the blizzard with the boat behind them, every step demanding great effort. The kobluna leader told them by gestures that their ships had been crushed by ice. He begged for food, and the Inuit gave them a piece of whale meat before they continued their journey. When natives returned the following spring, they found 30 bodies under a boat that had been turned upside down for shelter, and a small silver plate engraved on the back: *Sir John Franklin, K. C. H.* (Knight Commander).

2.

I wrote to scientists and expedition leaders who crossed Greenland on dogsleds, begging them to take me with them as part of the crew. Greenland is covered by ice and snow, a giant desert without trees and plants. In winter, the island plunges into darkness for months on end.

As many as 80 percent of Greenlanders suffer from depression. The reason is not, as most people might assume, the long winters or the lack of sunlight. After all, the Inuit have adapted to the months of darkness. Yet throughout winter, families must gather inside the house, usually in a single room because the cost of heating is extremely high. It is too dark and too cold for anyone to go outside, and they must share the same room for months.

In these tight quarters, nobody talks about themselves. If they are exasperated, angry, anxious, or depressed, they never say a word. They suppress their voice, keep their mouths shut and their feelings blocked. As Andrew Solomon wrote in *The Noonday Demon: An Atlas of Depression*: ". . . the distinctive features of Greenlandic depression are not direct results of the temperature and light; they are the consequence of this taboo against talking about yourself." Their silence gets them through many dark winters and allows them to cope with the difficult problems of survival, but it comes with a devastating price. Suicide accounts for one-tenth of all deaths on the island, and the rate among young people is increasing, often tied to alcoholism and domestic violence.

In my research, I came across an old Romanian professor who trekked alone on a remote Norwegian island in the Arctic. I asked him to take me along on an expedition, but he always traveled alone. He trained throughout the winter in a park in Bucharest by pulling a heavy truck tire behind him by a rope wrapped around his waist. He camped on ice and slogged against snowstorms so heavy that they resembled walls closing in on him from all directions. He told me how one morning, before dawn, he woke to the thunder of a glacier crashing in the sea below. The chunk of ice shattered the water and started an avalanche a few hundred feet beneath him. He described polar bears roaming in the distance, looking for prey.

I applied to university programs in the Arctic, wrote to research centers, contacted shipping companies, and reached out to polar institutes, but nobody responded. I ran out of ideas and, in the end, gave up on the north.

3.

After a month of trying to make my way north, I called one of my friends. "This is not working," I told her. "I tried everything!" We sat down for dinner in a café in the old town of Bucharest and clinked our glasses against a backdrop of blues music. She took a sip of red wine, looked me straight in the eyes, and smiled.

"You're ugly when you whine," she said. "Stop it. Wouldn't you rather look back a year from now and see 365 days of trying, stumbling, failing and falling, rather than a yearlong metro ride, home to work, work to home?"

"I guess," I said.

For the next six months, I jumped on the train before the 8 A.M. crowd. I did my research about the South Pole before my colleagues came in the office, then worked on my aerospace software during the day. In the evening, after everyone left, I put my feet up on the windowsill, pulled the laptop on my lap, and wrote to whomever I believed might get me to Antarctica.

I applied for jobs on cruise ships to work as a sailor or helper in the kitchen. They rejected me. I wrote letters to every polar institute in the world, and asked for a job that would take me to the South Pole. No one replied. I wrote NASA and asked them to take me on one of their flights to McMurdo Station, the United States Antarctic base. No one answered my e-mail, but they probably had a good laugh in the office.

I began writing a proposal for a research project to get funding from the Romanian government and the European Union. They said I was too young, and I didn't have enough experience or the required scientific background. Somebody explained that even if I'd met all the requirements, the process would take seven years. Furthermore, I would have to pay for the project myself and later get a refund from the government. "That's the dumbest thing I've ever heard," I told that person. "If I could pay to go to Antarctica, I wouldn't be working my butt off writing proposals. I would just go."

I joined polar associations for students, and they welcomed me on their teams. I soon realized why: they put me to work as a volunteer to find funding so that *they* could travel to Antarctica. I ran away from them as if a polar bear were after me.

Six months and thousands of letters later, not one single answer. My hope bucket was almost drained.

4.

As Rumi wrote seven centuries ago, the breeze at dawn had secrets to tell me.

I opened my eyes in the dead of night. The numbers of the clock on the nightstand flipped to show 3:05 A.M. In ancient spiritual traditions, this time of night, a few hours before dawn, is known as the sacred hour. The city noise is low, the ego is sleeping, the mind is quiet and open to insights that come from the Holy Spirit. *All the roads you have taken so far to reach Antarctica led you nowhere because your thinking went against your heart and you acted opposite to your nature,* said the voice in my head. *You're going in the wrong direction, contrary to your calling. This is why nothing is working.*

The truth was I didn't really want to spend the days with my head in the sink scrubbing dishes, or to be thrown by waves from wall to wall in a dark engine room. I didn't want to roam the hallways of a polar research station for six months with no way of going home, and I definitely didn't want to lock myself in a government contract and throw away the key for seven years. I just wanted to travel and explore the nature, to breathe in the polar wind, and to walk in the beauty of the end of the world.

My eyes suddenly lit upon the camera on my dresser. For more than a year, I'd tucked bills underneath my sweaters in the dresser, until I'd saved enough to buy a beginner photographer's camera. I read every book I found on the craft and walked the streets of Bucharest with my plastic camera dangling from my neck. I photographed people and pigeons, light poles, children, and empty benches in the park. I shoved my camera in my friends' faces and photographed their zits, pores, and nose hair, and pulled it away just before they smacked me.

As the saying goes, "The best hiding place is in plain sight." In spite of my passion for photography, the idea to travel to Antarctica as a photographer never lit up in my brain until now.

As soon as the numbers of the clock on my nightstand flipped to 7 A.M., I jumped out of bed and onto the train. "This is your last chance," I said to myself as I rushed through the office. I threw my feet on the desk, pulled my laptop on my lap once again, and wrote a letter to all companies that operated cruise ships to Antarctica. The story: *Romanian student to create a photographic album of the South Pole to raise awareness on climate change. I will offer you the photo album for taking me on board.* I signed my name, and hit the send button more than 100 times before lunch.

5.

In 1907 Norwegian explorer Roald Amundsen began writing down his plans to be the first expedition to reach the North Pole. As a boy, he had been fascinated by the stories of polar explorers. "What appealed to me was the suffering they endured. A strange ambition burned in me to experience those same sufferings," wrote Amundsen in his autobiography, *My Life as an Explorer.*

Explorer Fridtjof Nansen, a friend of his, agreed to lend his ship, *Fram.* Amundsen spent two years finalizing the expedition plans, but before he could set sail, American Robert Peary became the first man in history to reach the North Pole. So Amundsen changed his plans in secret and sailed south instead. He refused to tell anyone about his new route—not even Nansen knew. When they raised anchor from Oslo, only four members of the crew knew the truth. Not until they docked on the Portuguese island of Madeira, close to the shore of Africa, did Amundsen tell his men that they were in fact sailing south.

The crew spent a year in a wooden hut they built on the shore of Antarctica. In the spring, five men, including Amundsen, took a path no other explorer had taken before, journeying into the unknown. Huskies pulled them on skis. "The breath of men and dogs freezes the moment it hits the air," wrote Amundsen in his diary. Snowstorms created solid walls of ice around them. The wind stabbed through cracks in their clothes. "It was sheer madness. We were running blind over unknown ground," wrote Amundsen.

After the men climbed the last of the highest glaciers of their journey, they set camp. According to plan, the sledge drivers killed most of the dogs, skinned them, and fed them to the men and to the other dogs. Amundsen remembered, "There was depression and sadness in the air—we had grown so fond of our dogs."

On December 14, 1911, their compass showed they had arrived. Amundsen's dream to be the first in history to conquer the South Pole had become reality. They put their hands together and thrust the Norwegian flag into the ice. "Victory awaits him who has everything in order—luck, people call it. Defeat is certain for him who has neglected to take the necessary precautions in time; this is called bad luck," wrote Amundsen in his account of the expedition, *The South Pole.*

6.

For two weeks, I stared at my in-box first thing in the morning, as well as every other minute of the day. It was the last thing I looked at before I turned off the lights, and I even checked it when I woke up in the dead of night. From the more than 100 e-mails I sent, I got two replies, both saying, "Not interested."

One Friday evening, I hopped on the train, and three hours later I was having dinner with my parents in my childhood apartment. I hadn't told them about my plans to go to Antarctica. I couldn't share my sadness that nobody had answered my letters. *It's probably time to give up*, I thought as I was washing the dishes. I lay in bed in my little room in the dark and looked at the ceiling with my hands under my head. *At least I tried . . .*

Again, I woke up at 4 A.M. and turned on my computer to look at an empty in-box. I was about to go back to sleep, when an e-mail appeared: "Hello, Dragos. We would love to have you on board. Please select your preferred departure date, and be in Ushuaia, Argentina, the day before. We will be departing from there to Antarctica. Best regards, Maria."

I stretched my eyes wide-open with my index fingers and thumbs, and read the e-mail again. And again, just to be sure. I jumped on my toes whispering *yes* over and over, like a teenager who was about to get lucky. My parents were still sleeping in the other room, so I expressed my joy as quietly as possible, gleefully dancing without my feet leaving the carpet. I did not go back to sleep. I lay in bed with my legs crossed, palms on my heart, and a big smile on my face.

I was going to Antarctica as a photographer.

CHAPTER 8

WHEN SHEEP TAKE OVER YOUR MIND

Try, fail, curse, suffer, get up and get moving,
master the skills you need, do the work, but be careful
who you tell. Secrets hold great power.

1.

After a three-hour drive, I sat down with my best friend in a coffee shop and proudly told him the news: I was going to Antarctica as a photographer.

"Give me a break," he said.

"What do you mean?" I retorted. "I just signed the contract with the company."

"Do you have money to go to Argentina?" he said.

"No . . ."

"You're not even a photographer." He laughed. "You don't have a professional camera. Your plastic toy will not make it in the cold."

My heart dropped in my stomach like a boulder into a puddle of mud.

2.

Sheeping (noun): *a state of mindlessly following others when in fact you know the truth and the right actions you must* *take, but you don't want to overcome social resistance, accept the brief emotional pain of going against social pressure, and assume full responsibility for your life.*

The dominant social force that drives our thinking and our actions is the unconscious *search* and *need* for social proof. In moments of uncertainty, when we are not sure what to do, we take our cue from others and accept their actions as the truth. We assume they know something we don't, and so we mimic their behaviors.

This process is unconscious and immediate. Social proof is the reason why it seems that a restaurant filled with customers has better food than an empty one. It's why we believe products with more reviews are better than those with fewer. It's why we go faster than the speed limit on the highway when all other drivers are doing the same. It's also why hundreds of people at a metro station might ignore and step over a man dying on the stairs. It's how a crowd of people can witness a violent crime with nobody intervening.

It's how airline pilots fly into thunderstorms and risk the lives of hundreds of passengers.

3.

On June 1, 1999, American Airlines flight 1420 was coming in through a storm for a night landing at Little Rock Airport in Arkansas. The cabin lights had been turned off, but the plane was illuminated by lightning that fenced in the aircraft from all directions. The plane convulsed, buffeted by winds. When the pilots tried to line up the plane with the runway, the storm changed directions several times, and then it suddenly thrust the plane down.

Passengers, rigid in their seats, clenched the armrests and screamed when the plane fell abruptly. Some of them prayed out loud. One of the passengers later said that he thought they were going to land on a wing.

The pilots were flying blind in the dark. They had to make a snap decision: try to land the airplane or go to another airport. Even with the darkness, the wall of rain, and storm clouds obscuring the runway, the captain decided to attempt to land.

The plane ricocheted out of control when it hit the tarmac. The pilots failed to brake, and the aircraft skidded off the end of the runway at more than 100 miles per hour, slamming into a steel walkway. The plane was ripped into pieces. The captain and ten passengers died in the crash. Passengers who were still alive scrambled to get out before the plane was engulfed by fire.

The cause of the incident was clear: flying into bad weather and pilot error during landing. The deeper investigators looked, the more they discovered evidence that flying into thunderstorms was a widespread habit among commercial airline pilots. Gregory Feith, principal investigator with the National Transportation Safety Board, said he was astonished to hear a recording of the incident in which the captain, an experienced pilot, says five minutes before landing, "I hate droning around visual at night in weather without having some clue where I am." He didn't know where he was, and yet he still went ahead with the landing. It was a recipe for disaster.

Following this incident, experts from NASA and MIT did a study on 2,000 airplanes to find out when pilots are more likely to fly and land in dangerous weather. The results shocked the entire industry: two out of three pilots flew and landed in thunderstorms. In the global context of increased competition between airline companies, crew members were under massive pressure to take passengers on time to destinations. Among other causes, the study revealed that pilots were more reckless if the airplane in front of them also flew and landed in bad weather.

4.

Sheeping is an unconscious psychological phenomenon: you follow the people around you and assume their behaviors even when you know the truth. You know the action you must take, but you don't want to overcome social resistance, accept the brief emotional cost of going against social pressures (usually anxiety), and assume responsibility for your life. What are others doing? What are they saying? What are they thinking? How are they behaving? In social contexts and circumstances of uncertainty, our brains mimic and mirror their thoughts and behaviors in automatic and unconscious ways.

Sheeping is the reason why your friends and family can be a hindrance to your dreams. Do they support you with your vision? When you have an idea, a new project, a start-up, there is a lot of uncertainty. Every beginning is unpredictable. The uncertainty can take years. The dream is very fragile, and it can fall apart at many levels. Keep your eyes only on your dream. Don't look at what others are doing; if people around you don't dare much in life, chances are you will imitate their behaviors.

If you are not careful, social proof can become the reason why you give up on your dreams. Most of the time, you start with just an idea and nothing else. You don't see the way. You don't know the steps you must take, and you have no clue what you are going to do next. The uncertainty is high as you walk into the unknown. At this point, you might start talking to your friends and family about your dreams. Oftentimes, in their most sincere attempt to help, they give advice without their full support. Then, you will adopt their ideas, adapt to their advice, and give up. Your own mind will crush your inspiration.

Close your eyes to the world, and don't look at what others are doing or saying. Keep your eyes on your dream. Talk to God, but not to people. Close the door to your room, leave the world outside, and pray in secret. Your spirit is the candle of God, and if your heart (not your pride or ambition) is lit up, trust the One who put the dream in your spirit. Don't tell anyone about your idea in the beginning. Work in secret. Do not talk about it. Try, fail, curse, suffer, get up and get moving, master the skills you need, do the work, but be careful who you tell. Secrets hold great power.

5.

I threw my empty cup on the table and left my friend in the coffee shop without saying a word. For several hours, I tramped through the city alone, staring at my shoes without blinking.

What am I doing here? These people agreed to take me aboard their ship. How am I going to honor the contract without a camera? What am I going to do? I stormed through alleys, murmuring to myself. "This was my only chance to go to Antarctica and I blew it."

I made my way into the office and found another message from Maria, the expedition manager. She said she was looking forward to us working together and had attached the contract signed by both parties. I needed to be in Ushuaia, at the southernmost tip of South America—the opposite side of the world for me!—a day before departure. The ship would be sailing from there to Antarctica.

From the fifth floor, I could see the colors of Bucharest, like red scars of light on the shadowy face of the city. The dust in the room was accumulating on the carpet, after long hours of floating aimlessly through the room, all day long, disturbed by the shoes of visitors. The servers were humming behind me.

I put my jaw in the palm of my hand and stared in the distance. "I guess it's too late to back down and change my mind," I said aloud. No other thoughts came for a long time. An image of a galaxy taken by the Hubble Space Telescope was whirling on the computer monitor in front of me, and reflected in my glasses: planets, comets, millions of glowing suns, stardust, and interstellar gas, all spinning around a black hole in the center.

The uncomfortable reality was clear: I was in Romania. I couldn't afford the plane ticket to Argentina. I had signed a contract. I had promised a photo album to the only people in the world who had opened the door to my dream and offered me a chance to go to Antarctica. I didn't have a camera to honor our agreement.

Fear dripped from my brain with each thought, from my forehead to the back of my mind, down my spine, and into my heart. *What do I do?* I wailed in my mind.

CHAPTER 9

THE BREATH OF LIFE

You are the light of the world.

1.

I doodled, lost in thought, staring off into the distance through my computer monitor. I traced the sketch of a galaxy on a piece of paper. The heart of the galaxy is a black hole, a point in space where gravity is so strong that not even light can escape. Because light cannot get out, nobody can see a black hole. Scientists know black holes exist because they are the center that holds everything together—planets, stars, stardust—in the galaxy. Galaxies are born, constantly change, and die. Just like galaxies, we are born, constantly change, and die. Our bodies change. Our minds change. Our emotions change. If everything about us changes moment by moment—body, thoughts, feelings, beliefs—then what are we? What is the center that holds our body, our thoughts, and our emotions together from the moment of our birth until our last breath on earth?

Nikola Tesla said: "One must be sane to think clearly, but one can think deeply and be quite insane." Don't believe a word you read. Think clearly. When you say "my body," you indicate a possession, something that you have. The "I" has a body. When you say "my mind," you indicate a possession, as well, something that you have. When you say "I think," the "I" is doing an action, is thinking. When you say "I feel," you have an experience. The "I" has the experience of emotion.

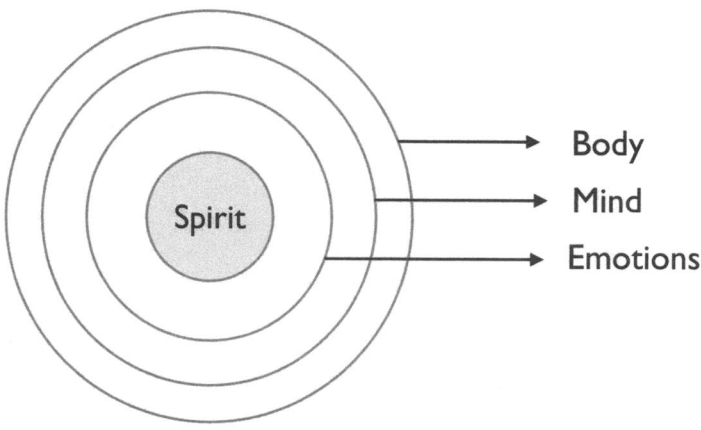

Since you cannot be a possession or what you have, you cannot be an action or what you do, and you cannot be an experience you're having or what you feel, the question then becomes: what are you?

The body that seems to be with us for a lifetime is in a constant process of change. Our bodies re-create themselves every seven to ten years. "We tend to think of our bodies changing only slowly once we reach adulthood. I was fascinated to discover that, in fact, we're changing all the time and constantly rebuilding ourselves," wrote Iris Schrijver, professor of pathology at Stanford University. Scientists estimate that our bodies are made of more than 37 trillion cells in an endless process of change.

Our body is like a river. When you sit on the bank of a river, you see a process that you know as a "river," but the river is never the same; it changes moment to moment. Our body is a process that follows a pattern, not an object. It changes all the time. As old stars die, galaxies renew themselves by pulling new stars from the universe. In the same way, our cells die and our bodies renew themselves by pulling new cells from nature, food, air, water, and the environment.

Our mind is constantly changing. Humanity has been trying to come up with a definition for the human mind for centuries, but we still haven't agreed on what the mind is. *Merriam-Webster* defines the word as "the element or complex of elements in an individual that feels, perceives, thinks, wills, and especially reasons." *Oxford Dictionary* defines it as "the element of a person that enables them to be aware of the world and their experiences." The Buddhist tradition defines the mind as a nonphysical continuum that perceives and understands the environment. The Christian tradition defines it as the God-given capacity of each person to think and reason. A scientific definition might say that the mind is a communication and control system between us and the environment.

The fact that definitions are not clear and do not agree is not important. What is important is the only point on which they do agree: the mind is an element, an instrument, a tool that we have to *use*, but is not what we *are*. Scientists developed new technologies to measure the frequency and intensity of thoughts, and to record images of the brain in various states of thinking. *Webster's Dictionary* defines thinking as the activity of using your mind to produce thoughts. Neuroscientists at the University of Southern California estimate that we have an average of 70,000 thoughts a day. From the darkest and the lowest to the highest and the lightest thoughts, our minds are in a continuous process of change.

Our emotions are constantly changing. In 1884 the father of modern psychology, William James, asked a question that has yet to find its answer: What is an emotion? The number of scientific definitions has grown to the point where even counting them is hopeless.

Paul Ekman, professor emeritus at the University of California, San Francisco, School of Medicine, is a pioneer in the study of human emotions and one of the most cited scientists of the 20th century. His mother committed suicide when he was a teenager, and this trauma drove him his entire life to find solutions to reduce human suffering. More than 40 years of scientific research showed Ekman that we have seven basic emotions that are innate and universal for all of us: anger, disgust, contempt, fear, sadness, surprise, and happiness. People in all cultures experience and show these emotions in the same way. Emotions come and go. They are not continuous experiences but discrete spikes that last for seconds or minutes.

Love is not among the innate emotions because love is not an emotion, Ekman revealed. While emotions are momentary, love endures for a lifetime. Love is the substance of what we are. All other emotions rise and fall on the foundation of love. For example, as a parent you love your child for life, and "you're most susceptible to experiencing a variety of emotions," wrote Ekman in his article, "Is Love an Emotion?" You can be angry with your children for something they've done, you can be annoyed when they don't listen, sad when they suffer, and happy when they are happy. You love them for life, regardless of how you feel in the moment. You love even when you don't feel anything. "Emotions don't endure, they come and go, lasting only seconds or at most minutes," continued Ekman. Our emotions are continuously changing. Love is the only constant.

When you observe a galaxy, you see planets, stars, and interstellar clouds spinning around a center that no one can see. The elements of a galaxy do not live forever. Planets, stars, and comets die and disappear, and others become part of it. The black hole in the center that no one can see holds everything together. When you observe yourself, you see your body, your thoughts, and your feelings spinning around a center that no one can see. These too do not last forever. Cells die and get replaced, thoughts come and go, emotions rise and fall. How can you be what in this moment *is* but is gone in the next, all the while you remain?

You are the spirit of God in an earthen vessel. The word *spirit* comes from the Latin word *spiritus*, which literally means "the breath of life." God's spirit living within you gives you life. The Bible says: "It is the Spirit who gives life" (John 6:63), and "In him was life, and the life was the light of men" (1 John 1:4). We are alive by the power of God within us. The Truth abides in us forever. This is why Saint Nicholas of Serbia wrote in the 1923: "Truth is not a thought, not a word, not a relationship between things, not a law. Truth is a Person. It is a Being which exceeds all beings and gives life to all."

When you become and remain aware of what you are in fact, you find the kingdom of heaven. The little sketch I drew revealed to me what Jesus meant when he said: "The Kingdom of Heaven is like yeast, which a woman took, and hid in three measures of meal, until it was all leavened" (Matthew 13:3). You are the life without polarity, and the love beyond the body, beyond the mind, beyond the emotions. You are the experiencer of all moments of your life. You are the light of the world.

You *are* God's son and daughter, and his spirit lives in you. The sun and the sunbeam, the vine and the branch, can never be separated. Only your thoughts and your actions can block your *awareness* of love. Jesus said: "I am the vine. You are the branches. He who remains in me, and I in him, the same bears much fruit" (John 15:5). The secret is to become aware of this reality, and live every moment from spirit and in Truth.

Apostle Paul wrote: "If I speak with the languages of men and of angels, but don't have love, I have become sounding brass, or a clanging cymbal" (1 Corinthians 13:1). This is the emptiness you feel within you when you don't honor the Truth and don't live from your heart. He continues: "If I have the gift of prophecy, and know all mysteries and all knowledge; and if I have all faith, so as to remove mountains, but don't have love, I am nothing" (1 Corinthians 13:2). Paul didn't write, "I *have* nothing," but "I *am* nothing." You are love, and when you do not love, you deny yourself.

2.

Dr. Kent Hoffman is a professor and clinical consultant at the University of Virginia. For 20 years, he's asked people from different backgrounds and social environments to describe the voices they hear inside their heads that they wish they didn't have to listen to. What one repetitive thought is constant in your mind that you would like to get rid of forever?

Regardless of whether he's working with a privileged group or the disadvantaged, the answer, he says, is almost always the same: "I am not enough." We struggle with "wounds of mattering."

If you've ever tried affirmations, those positive statements you repeat to yourself, you probably noticed some of them didn't work. You were just trying to tell yourself something you didn't believe. In this case, the conscious mind (the affirmation) goes against the subconscious mind (your beliefs). The most powerful affirmation doesn't come from the conscious mind, but from your spirit. With this affirmation, you are not trying to convince yourself of something you don't believe; instead, you are becoming aware of the truth and the reality of what you already are. The most powerful affirmation you will ever find is this: "I am as God created me."

Regardless of your circumstances, bring this idea to your awareness as often as possible. This thought comes directly from your spirit, and so bypasses all the beliefs constructed by your social environment. The voices of the world stand still when the voice of Truth speaks to you. "I am as God created me" includes everything: I am worthy, I am enough, I am loved, I am whole. There is no darkness in this thought, and it leaves no place for doubt. You are as God created you, unchangeable by all the moods and shifts in thinking, feeling, and beliefs, and with all the alterations in conditions of the body and the mind. Truth doesn't change; it doesn't need to be defended. All you must do is protect your awareness of the Truth.

3.

Back to my Antarctic trials. I decided to write a letter and title it "Student Goes on Expedition to the South Pole." I sent it to every single company in Romania that might lend me a professional camera: global brands, resellers, repair shops. I waited for two weeks, but nothing happened.

Finally, one day, a lady from the marketing department of a Japanese company with an office in Romania called me, saying that she wanted to meet during lunch. When the time came for our meeting, however, the taxi driver couldn't find the address, so he dropped me off outside the city, at the end of a bridge overlooking the railway. I could see the five-story building from there. "There must be so many cameras in there," I said to myself.

The sun above my head was so hot, it seemed to be melting the asphalt. I couldn't see a street, so I took off my suit jacket and ran through the brush. I jumped the railway, and got out on the other side in the parking lot, my shirt translucent with sweat. My hair, my socks, my pants, and my only pair of dress shoes were covered in thistles. I wiped my forehead with my sleeve and confidently walked into her office. I told her my story, smiled the way the books said to. After five minutes we shook hands, and she said she would call me.

By the time I got home, she had already sent me an e-mail apologizing that they didn't have any cameras. My only hope had just vanished. I sat down at the kitchen table, with my hands holding my hair and forehead, and looked through the vapor that rose from the cup of green tea in front of me. *What now?* I thought.

My childlike belief that had survived for half a year crumbled, and a grown-up's reality arose from its ashes.

4.

Love is the foundation, and love and life are one. Your body, your mind, your emotions are merely the tools you have been given to create and experience life. Science is finally revealing the way to use these tools to move the mountains in our lives.

As human beings, we come into this world with three extraordinary tools to create and experience life: body, mind, and love. To explain this, think of a coachman, a horse, and a carriage. The only way they can travel the distance and reach their destination is for the three of them to go in the same direction.

The coachman is your *mind*. He knows the direction, and must keep the carriage and the horse on the road. He can hold the reins and guide them to destination, or he can lead the horse and the carriage off a cliff.

The horse is your *love*, the energy of life. You can go all the way only if you are pulled by love, the only real power. If you are driven by your emotions, you will not go far because they are nothing more than momentary spikes of energy.

The carriage is your *body*. It doesn't move without the coachman and the horse. In the pursuit of dreams, you cannot have inner conflicts. You cannot think you want to go left, feel you want to go right, and then walk forward, because you will end up going nowhere. The path you have chosen must be traversed with the body, the mind, and the heart as one.

In the 1990s, cellular biologist Dr. Glen Rein organized a series of experiments at HeartMath Institute in California to see if people can influence matter using only their thoughts and emotions. Rein had 10 practitioners who were trained to feel love and heart-centered feelings of appreciation, gratitude, and compassion. He asked them to hold a sealed tube containing a sample of DNA for two minutes. They were then divided into three groups. The first group self-generated in their hearts elevated emotions of compassion and gratitude, but had no clear intention in their minds to change the DNA. They found that the statistical change in the DNA was insignificant.

The second group held a focused intention to wind or unwind the DNA, but were instructed to not enter into an elevated emotional state. They only focused their minds on the outcome. Nothing happened to the DNA tubes of this group.

The third group of participants held a focused intention in their minds to wind or unwind the DNA, and felt in their hearts love and elevated emotions of compassion and gratitude. In this case, the DNA strand changed up to 25 percent.

If the DNA in a sealed tube can change in two minutes by thought and love alone, just imagine what you can do if you focus your mind for years on what you love. Jesus said, "If two make peace with each other in this one house, they will say to the mountain, 'Move away!' and it will move away." When your mind and your love become one in your body, and you act toward your dream, even if the mountain doesn't move, you will have the power within yourself to climb the mountain all the way to the top.

5.

Not knowing what else to do, I opened the websites of photo companies from around the world, and I sent my letter through their contact form that surely nobody reads: "Student goes on expedition to the South Pole. Lend me a camera in exchange for a photographic album." I wrote to companies in Japan, the United States, Singapore, England, and Russia. Another two weeks later, my in-box still showed zero messages.

One morning, I woke up to my phone ringing at 8 A.M., with the lovely voice of a woman at the other end of the line. She introduced herself as the director of a Japanese company in Romania—the same company I had visited a while ago who had denied my request. She invited me to her office.

A few hours later, I walked through the door to see this unbelievably beautiful woman in her 30s, with a sweet smile that shined through her big brown eyes. On her desk there were two cups of fresh coffee and a golden box.

"Dragos, I have received your request for a camera, and we would love to support you," she said, pushing the box toward me. "Here's our latest camera with everything you need inside. It's the best in the world. Bring it back when you come home."

"Thank you!" I answered. I was at a loss for words. I took a sip of coffee.

"Congratulations for your expedition! We are proud to support your work," she said.

I cradled the box in my arms like it was a newborn baby as I walked toward the door. "If I may ask," I said, "why did you change your mind? I met one of your colleagues before, and she wasn't interested in my project."

She smiled as she sat down behind her desk. "Our corporate headquarters in Japan received the e-mail you sent through the contact form on their website. They liked the project, and sent a request to our office in Romania to sponsor you. Because the letter came from our global headquarters in Japan, we didn't really have much choice!" She winked at me.

"I am sorry . . ." I trailed off.

"This is my company, and I love your project." She laughed. "I'm glad you persisted and sent your e-mail to Japan. Otherwise, I would have never known you." We said farewell to each other with big smiles on our faces.

CHAPTER 10

THE FINAL BOARDING CALL

When you commit yourself to making
your dreams a reality, you will walk roads
that others will not see.

1.

Some of my prayers had been answered. A company had agreed to take me on board their ship. I had the golden box with the camera I needed inside. In a leap of faith, I decided to fly to South America a couple of weeks before the vessel was scheduled to leave the harbor. I spent $20 (a princely sum to me then) to reserve my spot at several hostels across Argentina, trusting I would somehow acquire the rest of the money I needed to pay for the rooms upon arrival. More important, I somehow had to find the money to fly over the ocean.

For several weeks, I reached out to travel companies in Romania with the same letter, asking if one would sponsor me with a plane ticket, or the money needed to buy one. I offered them the same photo album; I had nothing else to give. A family who owned a small travel agency eventually accepted and promised me $1,000 for the flight.

After 10 months of working for my doctoral studies during the day and on my expedition during the night, I had pulled it off. There was a giant smile on my face and a song on my lips as I pulled out my laptop to look for flights to Argentina. "Thank you, God," I said.

As I looked at the screen, the song disappeared from my lips. Sweat trickled from my forehead to crash onto the keyboard. In the time it had taken to find a sponsor, work out an agreement, fill out the paperwork, and await the bank transfer, the flight I needed had doubled in price.

For more than an hour, I looked at the monitor, not knowing what to do. Finally, I bought the only flight I could afford: a round-trip flight from Madrid, Spain, to Buenos Aires, Argentina. I prayed that I would find a way to get to Spain. After all, Madrid is only a four-hour flight away from where I was in Bucharest.

I spent the rest of the night under the blanket, asking God why this was happening to me. Why now, at the end?

2.

In 300 B.C., a man by the name of Zeno of Citium began teaching a new philosophy to the crowds that gathered at the colonnade, in the agora of ancient Athens. Zeno's way of looking at ourselves, at our place in the universe, and at our relationship with the world is known today as Stoicism.

Stoics understood that we do not have much control over the circumstances in our lives, but we do have complete control over how we think about them. Rational thinking always leads to inner peace, regardless of the environment. Errors in thought always create inner turmoil, regardless of the environment. People in dire straits can be peaceful and serene, and people with perfect lives can slump into the abyss of depression.

The mind is an instrument designed to keep us safe, not to make us happy. When it makes a decision about the future, the mind makes the situation a lot worse and predicts the outcome to be more disastrous than it will likely be. Sometimes things do not turn out for the best, but they often turn out better than we feared. Fear is not reality. Fear is an emotional consequence brought about by erroneous thinking. In moments of difficult decision making, Stoics followed the dark road to peace and tranquility, and embraced in their minds the worst-case scenario. What is the worst that can happen? If that happens, then what? What if I find myself in the worst possible outcome? Can I live with that?

Running from the thing you fear turns it into a dreadful monster. Facing the thing you fear, even if only in your mind before you make a decision, takes away your fear. When you define and embrace the worst possible outcome, you realize the darkest scenario is not so dark after all. The worst rarely happens.

"When a resolute young fellow steps up to the great bully, the World, and takes him boldly by the beard, he is often surprised to find it comes off in his hand, and that it was only tied on to scare away timid adventurers," wrote Oliver Wendell Holmes. When you embrace uncertainty, fear, or failure, they no longer hold you in chains. When you hide from them, they grow. When you grow, they hide.

If you quit your job to start a project that is meaningful to you, and it fails, what is the worst that will happen? It is inconvenient, but if it happens, what will you do? Are you not greater than this fleeting situation? If you lose your money trying to make your dream a reality, what is the worst that will happen? You will suffer for a while, feel angry or sad, unpleasant and inconvenient emotions will rise and fall, but eventually you will get through. The experience doesn't have to be horrific or terrible, unless you think of it this way.

3.

The contract with the shipping company was under a pile of books I had prepared for the journey. The camera was in the golden box on my desk. The trekking maps, a travel guide, and my bus tickets for Argentina lay scattered across the floor. The corner of a plane ticket from Madrid to Buenos Aires stuck out from under my laptop.

You really messed up this time, I thought, holding my forehead in my palms. *Who do you think you are to assume your dreams are possible? Look at what dire straits you're in now. You have to give* all *these people a photo album—the shipping company, the camera company, the travel agency. How will you pay back the money to the travel agency when they realize you can't go to Antarctica? The airline will not refund the money for the ticket. You will not be able to give anyone a photo album from your bedroom. You're not worthy of anything other than a low-paying job. You're nothing more than a dumb student.*

These voices became my only companions. They spoke to me when I woke up, and they waited under the covers when I tried to sleep. They murmured to me when I opened my eyes in the middle of the night. They whispered behind every conversation, talked in the gap between my thoughts, and shouted louder than traffic. They were the needle behind every sting in my body, the gasoline for every flare of anger, and the brushes that painted my life in the loneliest gray.

I stared out the window, but I couldn't see Antarctica anymore. Just the grim reality. The ship was setting sails for the South Pole in a few weeks, and I was in Bucharest without any money, ideas, or hope.

4.

One Friday evening in October, I was alone in the office when my phone rang. It was my doctoral adviser, the leader of the satellite image processing division with the German Aerospace Center. He was calling me from the airport, and his voice barely cut through the crackling, buzzing, and static. He told me that I needed to present at an upcoming conference. "I will see you in a week," he said, then hung up.

Damn, I thought, hanging up the phone. *It's not bad enough that I don't have money to fly to Madrid and I am going to lose the expedition, but now I have to fly to Frankfurt to present my research.* I stepped outside on the balcony to breathe in the crisp autumn air and make a decision.

If I don't go to this conference, I might lose my job and the chance to complete my Ph.D., I thought. Students had little room for negotiation. *At the same time, I might not find money for the flight to Madrid this week anyway, and then I won't go anywhere. I lose* everything. *If I go to the conference, then I forget all about Antarctica, but at least I get to keep my job.*

I called my adviser back, my heart in my throat. "I cannot present at the conference this month," I said. My hands trembled.

"Dragos." His words carried a chill, like a hailstone dropping down my back. "You must come. Your work has entered a research competition at the European Union Satellite Centre, and you must be there to present. Military, defense experts, and leaders of the space industry will be there."

"But—" I said.

"The conference is on the fifth of November. That's next week. We are holding it in Madrid this time. We made an exception and have already paid for your flight."

My eyes flashed to the ticket printout underneath my laptop: "Booking confirmed. Economy Class. Departure: Friday, 6 NOV, Barajas International Airport, Madrid. Arrival: Friday, 6 NOV, Ezeiza Ministro Pistarini International Airport, Buenos Aires."

"I'll be there!" I said.

5.

Before he sailed to the South Pole, Roald Amundsen spent the polar winter among the Inuit people on an island at the North Pole. Being the expedition leader, Amundsen was invited to share a dwelling with the *angakkuq*, the tribe's shaman and medicine man. Villagers often came to the angakkuq with their problems, but Amundsen could not understand how the shaman was actually helping them. One day he confronted him about his pretense. Didn't it bother him that his magic powers are nothing more than cheap tricks? Amundsen asked.

"My magic power is not in my tricks," answered the shaman. "My real power is that I have gone out on ice, and lived there alone for many months, until I could finally hear the voice of the Universe. And the voice of the Universe is that of a mother calling after her beloved children."

6.

When you live in Truth, surrender to the mystery, take a chance, make-believe, and refuse to give in, you will not receive what you think you deserve, but what you really want. When your pockets are empty, go where your heart is full because when you follow the love, even if your mind sees obstacles in the future, by the time you arrive there, the obstacles will have been removed for you.

Your heart doesn't care about being easy; your heart cares only about your living in Truth. When you commit yourself to making your dreams a reality, you will walk roads that others will not see. You will go through doors where others will see walls. When you hesitate, embrace your confusion and go for what you desire anyway. When you are afraid, embrace your fear, and still go for what you desire. When you lack faith in yourself, trust the voice of Truth, and keep doing the work anyway.

Uncontrolled thoughts will run through your head. Don't listen to everything you think. Insatiable fears will ripple through your body. Don't obey everything you feel. Listen to the voice of the Universe. The secrets the breeze at dawn has to tell you are to return to love, embrace the Truth, and trust the process to the very end.

7.

The morning our ship set sail for Antarctica, I discovered in my in-box an admission letter to a university program in the Arctic. I had applied to this program almost a year before, when I first started looking for a way to get to the North Pole. This expedition on a small Arctic island was to begin a few days after my return from Antarctica.

I stepped outside on the deck as we left the harbor and sat down under a blanket at the back of the vessel. The houses and the fishing boats on the dock became smaller and smaller. The ship sailed through the waves of the ocean, and the sky sparkled purple above the snow-covered mountains behind. A teardrop fell into a diamond of gratitude on my cheek, as the voice of the captain came through the speakers: "We are now passing Puerto Williams, the southernmost town in the world. Next time we see land, we will be in Antarctica."

I wrote back to the university in the Arctic, saying that I would be there for the program. I didn't know how I would find the money for this new adventure, but my childlike faith had returned. The whole world was beautiful. The wind carried from my lips a silent thank-you to the shores of Patagonia before they disappeared under the horizon.

8.

Two days later, we reached shore and disembarked. After a year of work, I had finally set foot in Antarctica. Waves sloshed on the rocks behind me. I took a few steps, and the snow crunched beneath my boots. My lips were cracked and my skin tingled with the sharpness of the wind blowing in my face.

Hundreds of penguins shuffled toward me, their squat, tuxedo-clad bodies wobbling from side to side. Their faces seemed to grin at me. To my left, a couple of penguins slid on their bellies and dove off a block of ice with a splash, like kids on a water slide, straight into the sea. Others clapped their flippers and made noises that sounded like laughter.

I put my hands on the camera hanging from my neck and felt the cold biting my fingers. I knelt to take a photo of the landscape and started laughing in joy. If home is truly where your heart is, then I was home. I had arrived.

PART III

WALK IN TRUTH

*Start by doing what is necessary, then
what is possible, and suddenly you
are doing the impossible.*

— SAINT FRANCIS OF ASSISI

CHAPTER 11

HIMALAYAN CANDY

*These four words are enough to make his dreams
come true. Why don't you learn from him?*

September 2013. Nepal.

1.

As the night embraced the Himalayan peaks behind me,
I bowed my head and walked through the narrow gate
of a Buddhist monastery in Nepal. The light of the sun
lingered to cast the shadow of the mountain against the
crimson walls of the temple. The Tibetan wheel of karma
and the two golden lamas on the roof disappeared behind
the veil in the dark.

I stood under a lamppost, the only pool of light in the
garden, trying to read from my travel guide and figure out
where I was. A few kids ran back and forth between buildings, carrying papers. With their simple robes, they looked
like they'd been tossed into sacks but had managed to get
their hands and head out and run.

It was the end of autumn, and my breath turned into
white clouds under the pale yellow light. The sound of
me flipping through the pages, the crackling prayer wheel,
and my footsteps on the crushed stone in the garden

created a rhythm that reverberated through the stillness of the night. The bark of a stray dog in the distance and children laughing in the village added music from beyond the monastery gates.

The wind brought from the top of the mountain the cold smell of Himalayan snow. I patted the heads of the two stone dragons that guarded the stairs to the temple, and walked toward the only building that still had a pale yellow glow coming from the windows. I wiped the glass with my sleeve and stuck my face against its cold surface to take a peek inside. In the classroom, Buddhist children gathered in groups of three around candle lamps to read. Their bodies were wrapped in traditional crimson robes that left out their shaved heads to shimmer in the lamplight. A monk was sitting in silence at his desk in front of them, fingering a string of wooden prayer beads.

Suddenly I felt something pulling my backpack. I turned around but didn't immediately see anyone. I looked down to find an elfin Buddhist kid, probably around four years old, staring up at me with sparkling eyes and a smile that stretched across his face. "Do you have candy?" he asked me, petting his tummy and licking his upper lip. His tiny black eyes glittered with joy.

"What's your name?" I asked him as I attempted to put down my backpack.

"Do you have candy?" he asked me again, smiling, holding my hand that held the backpack. I sent my other hand on a hunt through my clothes to find candy for him. He munched the chocolates I handed to him, then took my hand and walked me to the abbot of the monastery without saying another word.

"He doesn't speak English," said the abbot, laughing from the doorstep. "Come in, please."

I sat in a bench in the same classroom I had looked in through the window earlier, and the abbot sat in front of me at the teacher's desk. He was probably in his 50s, and looked like the Laughing Buddha statue. Every sentence he said ended with his laughter echoing in the garden. I had come to the Himalayas to learn more about myself and about the Buddhist spiritual traditions, and so I asked him what was his life story and why he became a monk.

When he was five years old, he said, he ran away from Tibet to escape the Chinese oppression. His family was left behind. He fled from the village, and crossed the mountains with some strangers who dropped him off in Nepal. He found refuge in a Buddhist monastery in Kathmandu, where he became a monk. He's been studying since then, and he was now traveling the world teaching Buddhism. His eyes shone with tranquility and joy.

"How come you're so happy?" I asked him.

"I meditate," he said.

After a minute of silence, he burst into laughter.

"You all come here hoping to find the secret to happiness, don't you?" he said. "Where you come from," he continued, "you have everything you need to have a happy life. You are free. We don't have that here. You can buy everything you need. You have access to an abundance of information. You have so much knowledge that your brain is drowning in it. Bookstores, libraries, Amazon, Wikipedia, everything you want on demand, literally at the tips of your fingers. Two girls who stayed here for a week showed me their apps for meditation. Why would you need that? I just sit down, close my eyes, and meditate. That's it!"

He paused for a minute and then laughed again, holding on to his belly. "You know what the problem really is? You fill your head with so much information, so much knowledge, so much stuff, but you never put it into practice. You never act on what you know. You never do it. You read about meditation, but you never sit down and actually do it." He laughed again.

"You read an article a day on how to meditate," he continued. "You learn the techniques. You go to evening classes on meditation. You read ten books on meditation. You buy a meditation pillow. You play meditation music. You download meditation programs with special brain waves. You get the latest app that sends you notifications to remind you to meditate. You try it a couple of times, and then you give up, change, and try something else. You never put in practice what you already *know*. You never do it long-term, and of course it's not working."

"I spent three years under a solitary tree in a park, praying every day," I said. "I had the peace of God, but then I stopped and lost it."

The abbot replied, "You read books on spirituality, and you feel you're the main character, or you want to make love to the main character. You read the sayings of the Buddha and buy a little copper Buddha. You buy a cat made in China that waves its hand to bring you luck. You light incense that your partner hates. You buy rocks. You buy a dreamcatcher. You get a tattoo with a dreamcatcher. You hang crystals around your neck. You smoke pot. You join a church. You don't agree with what the pastor is saying, and go to the church across the street. You go to India to get blessed by your guru. You chant. You save money to fly to South America to throw up in front of a shaman. You try to find your luck in numbers, in coffee, or in the stars. You read your horoscope in the morning. You come to my temple in Nepal. You shave your head. You grow dreadlocks. You speak to yourself in the mirror. You post spiritual quotes online. You freak out your relatives by telling them you want to quit your job and move to an organic farm. You go on a retreat. You hug horses. You hug strangers. You take pills. You cancel sex—too much sex. You have sex—then send your partner a questionnaire about how you can improve your sex. Aren't you tired of looking for solutions outside, where they cannot be?

"You must understand something. Everything you're doing, you're doing because you are trying to escape fear and find peace. To forgive and be forgiven. To love and be loved. To find meaning and a sense of purpose in life. How can you find the solution outside yourself when it is inside you? You don't need to travel to the other side of the world to find yourself; you have everything you need within. Sit down and meditate. You are solely responsible to rule your mind, and you must rule it alone. Meditate. Do the work. Pray every single day, and you will find peace."

He gave me a serious look and burst again into laughter.

"Have you seen how happy this child is, the one you've just met?" the monk asked. "He gets free candy and chocolate every day. He knows only four English words, and he speaks them to every tourist he sees: *Do you have candy?* Every day, the same words. For him, these four words are enough to make his dreams come true. He never misses a day. Why don't you learn from him?"

This time we laughed together.

He continued, "You read books that tell you that if you want to be fulfilled in life, you have to follow your heart and make a contribution in the lives of others. You make notes on the side, underline key sentences with a yellow highlighter, nod in agreement with your head between the pages, but you never put it into practice. You don't live what you read. What do you do? You put the book down and do the exact opposite. In the process, you also think of reasons why what you've just read applies to others, but not to you. And the more you read and the more you study, the more you think that nothing is working. You try something for a few days, but you don't apply it long-term, which is what really makes the difference.

"This gap between what you *know* and what you *do* is driving you crazy, because your mind and your actions are in conflict. It's that simple. Sit down. Meditate. Don't think about it. Don't talk about it. Whatever it is that you must do, do it."

2.

In the years that followed, this conversation with a Buddhist monk ran in my mind over and over. It opened my eyes to the fact that I hadn't actually taken much action toward my own dream. I'd thought about it for a long time, spoken about it, told others to follow their dreams, imagined myself doing it one day . . . But that was it. All talk and not so much work.

I had read the books, watched the films, and filled my head with all the information. The reality was I was still in the same old job, doing the same old thing; nothing was different in my life. It was time to get to work.

CHAPTER 12

BEFORE EVERYTHING HAPPENS, WE MUST FIRST BEGIN

*They will dismiss your idea,
and they will dismiss you.*

October 2013. Italy.

1.

When I returned to Romania from my trek in the Himalayas, I made the decision to change my life. The success of my expeditions years before to the North and the South Poles had given birth to a new dream for me: to empower people to make their dreams a reality even if they start with very little. If a shy, below-average student from Romania could fulfill his dream to explore the Arctic and the Antarctic by himself alone, to complete a doctorate degree in the field of satellite image intelligence, to be the engineer of a space simulation mission that paved the way for future human missions to Mars—well, then, *anybody* can live their dreams, no matter who they are or where they start from.

I traveled to Italy for a few days, and visited with my team from NASA and the International Space University in the sacred temple of pizza, as L'Antica Pizzeria da Michele was called, in the center of Naples. The recipes of this famous place have been kept secret since 1870, and people from all over the world elbowed their way in to taste a slice of the traditional *pizza Napoletana*. We gobbled down our pizzas and shared a few memories from our time at NASA.

"We should write a book to inspire students to study science," the professor said in his French accent.

"Nobody will read an overpriced academic book about science and education," I said to all sitting at the table. "If we want to make an impact, let's make a movie and go global."

After we finished our last slices of pizza and elbowed our way out of the restaurant, I raised my voice to overcome the hubbub of laughter and shouting in the street. "Let's bring NASA legends, rock stars, renowned authors, and entrepreneurs to show people how they can make their dreams a reality!" I said. "Does anybody here know how to make a film?"

Everyone shrugged their shoulders. We chattered happily all the way back to the hotel, and we made plans for what we were going to do next. Thus, the idea for *The Amazing You* movie was born.

November 2013. Bucharest.

2.

Three days after our conversation in Naples, everybody had flown back to their home countries and was back at their jobs. I contacted everyone, eager to keep the momentum on the film going. Most never wrote back.

I was once again in my office in Romania, living the same rhythm as years before: I woke up around 9 A.M., squashed my body in a crowded subway, read a book on my way to work, grabbed a plastic cup of green tea as I walked in the office, and crashed into my chair—this time, trying to figure out how to make a movie.

I continued to work in the space industry for a while, doing research during the day, but the voice of the Universe was calling me again. Most nights, lunch breaks, free moments, and weekends found me at my desk, working on the film. I had no idea where to begin, so I wrote down ideas, concepts, and chapters, questions, stories, and creations. I talked to friends, but mostly to myself. I scratched my head and wrote letters to people. I inspired others and encouraged them, annoyed them and upset them. I didn't know what to do, so I did whatever crossed my mind to learn and move forward.

3.

I am nobody, I thought to myself. But just like "I am afraid," "I am nobody" by itself doesn't mean anything. The hidden meaning, and what you do after you had the thought, is what actually matters. "I am afraid" can be the end or the beginning: "I am afraid, so I will run away," or "I am afraid, and I will embrace my fear and do it regardless."

I am nobody, I thought to myself. *I am a student from Romania with absolutely no track record of making movies.* All I had was a one-page document describing the film. And thus I began.

From behind my tiny desk in my office in Bucharest, I reached out to Dr. Dorin Prunariu, the only Romanian cosmonaut and chairman for space at the United Nations, and asked him if he would do an interview for my film. He flew into space years ago, and now he supports young people from all over the world to follow their dreams. He said yes.

I then wrote to NASA and invited several people to do a short interview for my film, which now, I told them, included "leaders from the United Nations, and other celebrities to be confirmed in the future." Only Prunariu had accepted my invitation, but nobody knew that. Before everything happens, we must first begin by telling a great story, and *then* do what we promise.

I got yeses from Dr. Charles Pellerin, the NASA legend who led some of the greatest scientific programs in history, and Dr. Ed Hoffman, the expert responsible for developing the leadership of NASA. I added their names to the letter.

I then reached out to Dr. Scott Hubbard, professor at Stanford University, and invited him to give an interview for my film, which now included "leaders from NASA, the United Nations, and other celebrities." Dr. Hubbard led the team that landed the three famous rovers *Spirit*, *Opportunity*, and *Curiosity* on Mars. He accepted.

I added NASA, United Nations, and Stanford University to my letter, and then wrote to Silicon Valley entrepreneurs, including one of the founders of the wildly successful game *Angry Birds*. Some said no—but some said yes.

The Japanese poet and Buddhist priest Issa once wrote: "O snail, climb Mount Fuji, but slowly, slowly!"

4.

In any project, from pitching your start-up to investors, to raising money for your nonprofit, to developing a multimillion dollar company that will extend human life or build the latest spacecraft, you need people on your side to support you. Everybody has a great idea. There are millions of great ideas out there, but it's *how* you execute your idea that is important. The best way to reach out to somebody with your idea is to rise above the line of *supercredibility*.

(I learned this from Dr. Peter Diamandis and Dr. Robert Richards, the founders of Singularity University and the International Space University.)

In our minds, we have a personal line of credibility: what we accept and believe is true. Ideas fall either below or above our line of credibility. If your idea seems too far out there, and you have absolutely no track record of success when you reach out to people, you will fall below the line of credibility. They will dismiss your idea, and they will dismiss *you*. If your idea falls above the line of credibility, they might give you the benefit of the doubt and continue to ask questions.

We also have a personal line of supercredibility. When an idea falls above this line, people immediately embrace it and back it up. Your ideas must fall above the line of supercredibility. You don't need a huge track record, you can be a student, but you must build your way up and present yourself above the line of supercredibility. Nobody expects you to have everything mapped out from the very beginning, but you must rise above the line of supercredibility by showing how you'll execute your idea, and that other people already believe in you.

When I finally sent my letter to rock stars and celebrity authors, it wasn't just Dragos, a doctorate student from Romania with an idea to make a film. I had lined up NASA legends and astronauts, leaders from the United Nations and Stanford University, the founder of Singularity University and the International Space University, Peter "Mighty Eagle" Vesterbacka from Angry Birds, and others. They endorsed my project through their mere presence.

Every step you take toward the top is possible because of all the little steps you took in the past. You can climb the mountain, but do it slowly, slowly.

CHAPTER 13

HOLES IN YOUR POCKETS

I stuck with my dream and paid the price.

January 2014. The West Coast of the United States.

1.

With the help of my close friends, the idea of the film started to take form on paper. For almost half a year, we worked day and night, in every spare moment we found outside our jobs. My best friend, Stefan, was crammed next to me in the chair in my one-room apartment in Bucharest. We stared at the computer monitor, wondering whether we should go ahead and book our flights to Florida. I had scheduled some meetings and interviews for the movie, but now it was time to put my money where my mouth was, and spend what I had been saving throughout the whole year.

"You will probably regret it in the future if you don't do it now," said Stefan.

I clicked the buy button.

2.

On our way to Florida, the airline cabin re-created the atmosphere of Antarctica, the cold wind piercing through the cracks in our clothes. When we landed in the heat of Miami, we felt like chicken pieces that had been taken out of the freezer and thrown into the oven.

We filmed an interview at NASA Kennedy Space Center, and then flew to Phoenix, Arizona. We landed around midnight without any clear plans; we just rented a car and drove north. When I could no longer keep my eyes open, we pulled into a motel by the side of the road. The middle of nowhere was just across the street. When we closed the doors to the car, all we could see was nothing, just a few stars above. In front of the motel was a giant cactus, the first I've seen in my life.

At our motel room, Stefan and I looked at the red-brown stain on the pavement in front of the door, then at each other, and then back at the stain, but we didn't say a word. *It's probably not what it looks like*, I thought. We blocked the door with the chair and our backpacks, and turned off the lights.

We had breakfast in an Amish diner, drove to the Grand Canyon past a giant statue of the Flintstones, and then drove straight to Los Angeles. Private companies test spacecraft in the Mojave Desert, but all we saw were colorful freight trains with no beginning and no end, winding through the California hills.

We walked around downtown L.A. in the morning, filmed interviews at noon, and had a fast-food dinner in Hollywood. Hollywood Boulevard looks like the lost-and-found office of the showbiz world. Aliens, Superman, Spider-Man, Mickey Mouse, Elvis, Marilyn Monroe, and all the characters you can think of mingle on this street, posing for photos for a tip. We saw people dressed as aliens, and aliens dressed as people, but we couldn't tell them apart.

We drove up north to the Bay Area. We filmed an interview at NASA in Silicon Valley in the basement of an old building, with pipes running above our heads and hot water dripping in the background. We filmed another on the perfect verdant campus of Stanford University.

In San Francisco, our credit cards went into the red. Every other day, Stefan woke up before sunrise to ask friends from Romania to send us some money. He asked different people on different days for the same $100 we needed to get through the moment.

January 2014. Bucharest.

3.

After we returned to Bucharest, I asked another friend to film my own interview for the movie. He had recently closed down his studio, but he invited me to his home to improvise something.

He didn't have a spare room in his little two-room apartment on the ninth floor. The living room was full of cardboard boxes as they'd just moved in, and his wife and daughter were sleeping in the bedroom. We had only one choice: film in the kitchen.

We hid the sink, the washing machine, and the stove behind a black paper backdrop. Because we couldn't raise the backdrop too high, I sat for 14 hours before it on the legs of a tiny wooden chair turned sideways. The lights burned the room and scorched my hair. But we filmed.

Their cat walked in front of the camera whenever she felt like it. Every other take was broken by sudden knocks, mysterious groans, strange pops and cracks, loud humming and whirring from the fridge. The video camera didn't fit in the kitchen, so my buddy filmed cloistered in a square-foot pantry, under a pile of winter clothes, assaulted by a thousand shoes around him. When the clock struck midnight, we ordered pizza because the fridge door was blocked by lights, chairs, cables, and tripods.

We got the job done.

4.

Before we'd flown to the United States to film the interviews, my friends and I agonized for months over all the little details of the movie. We wrote proposals to raise money, hundreds of pages of script, ideas, and possible scenarios. But things changed after we returned home. Whenever we planned to meet and work, I was more often than not the only one to show up.

Spring turned into summer, into autumn, into winter. My friends got busier with other projects. The spark of their enthusiasm dimmed, then eventually went out. I stuck with my dream and paid the price. I found myself broke and alone.

Bucharest was covered in brown slush and dirty ice for most of that winter. Romanians dawdle until roads turn completely white, and then plowing machines push all the snow on the sidewalks. Walkways become useless. High school students in uniforms, businesspeople in suits, women in skirts, dogs, and old ladies climb the mountains of gray snow on all fours. They walk in the road and jump in front of the cars that honk and curse but can't brake.

Most evenings found me rambling alone through deserted alleys in the park or slogging through slush in the old city, looking at all the other people smiling and cheering in the windows of restaurants. *How did I get here?* I thought. *Will I ever rebuild my life?*

I'd lost everything. The holes in my pockets had grown to the point where I had to choose between buying warm winter boots or shivering and sliding in my old sneakers in the snow so I could put all my money into the film.

I chose the latter.

CHAPTER 14

HOLES IN YOUR HEART

Life is never made unbearable by circumstances,
but only by lack of purpose.

January 2014. Bucharest.

1.

The wind that comes from Siberia makes nights in Bucharest particularly cold during winter. The river sometimes stops flowing and freezes over. Icicles hang from every building, and locals put warning signs to alert people of the imminent danger growing above them.

I had just finished filming the interview in my friend's apartment and was on my way home. The clock on my phone showed 3:10 A.M. The taxi dropped me off five minutes away from the building because he couldn't drive through the slush ditches that covered the alley. A man and a woman muffled in rags were looking through the garbage bins with a flashlight. When I passed them, the lady jumped in front of me, rubbing her tattered fingerless mittens.

"Do you have a blanket for us?" she asked. "We are freezing out here." The cracks in her skin, and the drops of blood on her lips, had turned black.

"I do," I said. "I will bring it to you the first thing in the morning. Meet me here." My girlfriend was sleeping, and I didn't want to turn on the lights in the room, and root around through the drawers and wardrobe at that hour in the night.

They thanked me and returned to the trash bin.

2.

My girlfriend and I had been together for six years. We met in college. She lived with me in the students' dormitory for a while, and after graduation I moved into her apartment. Our friends often said that we were the most beautiful couple. We never argued, and we never fought. For five years, we were children in love.

Like most youngsters in their 20s, however, we matured in different directions, with dreams that were poles apart. Neither of us recognized or accepted that we'd become different, and so we became distant. We couldn't accept the reality that we had grown apart, we ignored our feelings, and we suppressed our truth. For her, sadness turned into anger; for me, depression. She snapped at me for things she once found cute, and I withdrew more and more into solitude. We didn't find the power to let go of each other. I needed to leave, to be alone for a while, but I couldn't afford to pay rent in another place. So I stayed for another year.

Depression burned a hole in my stomach, like a branding iron burns the skin of a helpless animal. I walked past the cemetery in our neighborhood, staring at my feet but talking to the graves, cursing the dead and mumbling about how lucky they were to have escaped the pain of being alive. I often slammed the door behind me in rage and slogged through the city talking to myself. I thought about climbing on the roof of a building, throwing bricks at drivers, and even jumping off. I never did any of it, of course. I never threatened, hurt, or even talked to anyone. I kept my mouth shut.

Looking back, I realize that what saved my life in those dark moments was my deep connection to my heart. The storms were raging in my mind, the pain slashed my body, but beneath it all, my heart was telling me that all would be well.

I clung to my heart every day. Depression and desperation spread through my body like ink through blotting paper. I needed to find a place to move if I was to survive my depression.

3.

When I woke up the next day, the destitute couple was the first thing on my mind. I dug through the back of my wardrobe and found a blanket my mom had given me when I'd left for college many years before. I put it in a cardboard box with a winter jacket, two sweaters, a pillow, a pair of shoes, a bottle of wine, and some Christmas cookies, and made my way to the bus stop where I'd met the couple scavenging through the trash bins only hours before. They weren't there.

I stayed at that bench for half an hour, waiting for them. Then I walked around the neighborhood, pressing the box between my arms and my chin so the stuff wouldn't fall out. I trudged through parking lots and the alleys, then returned to the bus stop. No sign of them.

"Are you looking for a place to move?" inquired an old man waiting for the bus. Even in Romania, where people have giant, loving hearts, strangers don't usually ask such questions in a bus stop. "I have an apartment for rent, very inexpensive," he said.

"What?" I said. "Why do you ask me?"

"I saw you carrying this box with clothes around the neighborhood for the last hour, and I assumed you're looking for a place to stay. I have a one-room apartment, just a few stops from here." He told me the price, and it was almost half of the usual rental price in Bucharest. I could afford it. I wrote down his phone number and promised to call him.

A week later, I moved out of my girlfriend's apartment on a damned January evening, skidding my way in sneakers against the blizzard, dragging an enormous bag with the stuff I owned. To this day, I don't know what happened with the destitute couple, but I've learned that whatever you do for others in unconditional love, God will do for you. I never called the gentleman from the bus stop back. Instead, an old friend invited me to stay in his spare room for a while without paying rent.

I'd lost my girlfriend, our hopes together, and the ring that remained hidden in a drawer. Even though I'd invested my life into my film, I hadn't made any progress for almost a year. I decided to call my friends, and I asked each one why we were not working on the movie anymore. We'd begun this journey together a year before, and I needed to hear from them why they had pulled back without saying a word.

"Because *you* want to be in the film," they each answered. "Who do you think you are? You're nobody. You will wreck the film with your presence. We don't want you in the movie."

4.

Luca found me on a bench in the park, about a week after I'd moved into my new place. I was rubbing my hands on my jeans, trying to warm up. The trees, the walkways, the children's playground, and the bench beneath me were frozen that night.

Luca was an old friend. He was the one who'd offered me that armchair to sleep on during my first week in college, when I roamed the streets. His dad fled the country when Luca was just a little boy, and his mom passed away when he turned 14. Ever since, he'd been passed around between his feeble grandma, his aristocratic uncle, and other relatives who lived in a town he despised. When he turned 18, he ran away.

Almost every night, he took some kind of drug and drank his consciousness away till morning. He'd have a job for a few months and then go for days, sometimes weeks, without eating. I once found Luca sleeping on a bench in a park, with a loaf of bread tucked under his arm. I took him into my bunk bed in the dormitory, and I convinced my boss at the music shop to give him my job.

He had lived through violence; when we were in high school, a gang beat him close to death just because he was playing guitar to his girlfriend. He survived drug and alcohol abuse, loneliness, homelessness, depression, and despair. He was surrounded by many friends who loved him, but still he struggled with his demons for more than 15 years. We played in bands together, and like the older brother I never had, he taught me how to approach girls in bars. He had the perfect combination of good looks, a beautiful heart, and the kindest smile in the world. Every girl fell in love with him, and every person became his dear friend.

He invited me to walk with him along the still-frozen river in Bucharest.

"I wanted to make this movie to inspire people to follow their dreams, because when they come from the heart, dreams become a reality," I said. "I lost everything, and now my friends, whom I trusted the most, want me out of my own film!"

People passing by turned their heads to see what was going on.

"Why don't you just give up?" he said.

"If God was as good as people think," I cried, and clenched my teeth to hold back my tears, "he would have been here on earth, instead of sending us to struggle with this pain. I don't want to live in this universe anymore!" I kicked a pile of slush with my foot. "It seems like the universe stood up against me so that I don't finish this film."

"Listen," Luca said patting me on the back, "you want to empower people to make their dreams a reality even if they start with close to nothing, right?"

"Yes," I muttered.

"Tell me: do you want to be a cover band and play the songs of others, or do you want to write your own music and play your own songs? Because if you want to imitate other people, you can; it's easy. But then you are cheating yourself of your own potential to create something remarkable. So, do you want to speak from books, or do you want to be authentic, and speak the truth?"

"I want to be authentic," I said. "Why?"

"Well . . . You're not gonna like what I have to say next," he said, smiling. "You now have the perfect opportunity to prove in your own life that which you want to share with others. What are the fruits of your wisdom? How can you tell people they can make their dreams a reality when you have failed with yours? Until you demonstrate in your own life what you want to share with others, you don't deserve to write any books, make any movies, or speak on any stage. The universe seems to be against you now, because you must demonstrate in your own life that which you know to be true in your heart. If you don't do that, you will be just another cover band that nobody remembers the next day. Even worse, you'll be an impostor."

We'd been walking for more than an hour along the river. The blizzard stopped, and the night sky cleared out, but the frost bit harder from my toes. I peeked into my wallet and found only a few coins, not enough for a drink somewhere to get out of the cold.

"Let's go in here," said Luca, walking into a Catholic church. "We can sit down and warm up. Catholics like comfort and have benches." He laughed. (Christian Orthodox churches in Romania don't have chairs. People stand, sometimes for hours, during service.)

Nobody was inside except for a lady at the entrance who sold candles, rosaries, and calendars. She hovered her legs over the orange blaze of an archaic open-coil electric plate. Her lips were moving, but she made no sound as she read from a tiny prayer book. We shut the door behind us, and the noise of the city died out. We could hear only the water dripping in the font.

"A long time ago," said Luca as we sat down on a bench at the front, "the devil decided to sell his tools to whoever offered the most for them. One night, he opened the doors to his customers and exhibited his utensils: fear, hate, jealousy, envy, pride, avarice, sloth, and many more. Somewhere, in a dark corner of the room, was a very old and worn-out object that seemed to have been used since the beginning of time. It was the most battered but had the highest price of all. Somebody asked the devil what that instrument was, and why it was so expensive.

"'*Discouragement*,' the devil answered. 'It is so damaged because it is the one I use most often on people. It is so expensive because when all other tools fail, this one always works. I crawl into their hearts, and nobody notices. Once they get discouraged, they're mine. I do whatever I want with them. I've been using it since the first man and woman walked upon this earth. It works with everyone because when people get discouraged and lose hope, they blame God or themselves or the ones around them. There are many obstacles in life, people stumble and fall, but when they get discouraged and fall into despair, that's just me doing my job.'" Luca pointed at a painting of a demon dragging a man down into flames. "Our work is tested and proven in trials."

"I am failing while trying to do a movie on how to be successful," I said. "The devil must be laughing his tail off."

"People become great only in the face of adversity," Luca said. "There is no other way. Think about it: in fairy tales, the youngest son goes off to battle the dragon. In the Old Testament, David defeated Goliath. Mahatma Gandhi, a frail Indian man, stood up against the British army. Mother Teresa stood against poverty and suffering in India. Martin Luther King, Jr., stood up against racism.

"These people didn't overcome hardships in their own strength. They had the inner calling, and the power of God within them, to do what they were doing. We work together with God here on earth. We can do nothing by our own strength. The greater their destiny, the greater was the adversity against them.

"Do you know what Apostle Paul went through to preach the gospel?"

"No, I'm sorry. I haven't read the Bible," I said.

Luca took a Bible from one of the benches and started reading: "'Even to this present hour we hunger, thirst, are naked, are beaten, and have no certain dwelling place. We toil, working with our own hands. When people curse us, we bless. Being persecuted, we endure. Being defamed, we entreat. We are made as the filth of the world, the dirt wiped off by all, even until now' (1 Corinthians 4:11–13). 'I have been in travels often, perils of rivers, perils of robbers, perils from my countrymen, perils from the Gentiles, perils in the city, perils in the wilderness, perils in the sea, perils among false brothers; in labor and travail, in watchings often, in hunger and thirst, in fastings often, and in cold and nakedness' (2 Corinthians 11:26–27).

"I think you're not doing too bad," Luca said, laughing. "Your situation is easier."

He continued reading from the Bible, "'Therefore I take pleasure in weaknesses, in injuries, in necessities, in persecutions, in distresses, for Christ's sake. For when I am weak, then am I strong' (2 Corinthians 12:10).

"No man can go through such hurt in his own strength. Do you imagine when Paul was having stones thrown at him or being chased and beaten, he was thinking, *I am writing the most influential book in the history of humanity?* No! He had a calling in his life, and God's purpose was greater than his suffering. It's not God who inflicted the wretchedness upon him; other people did. God was with Paul always, to give him power to fulfill his mission in spite of the circumstances. Paul will never know it, but hundreds, even thousands of years later, generations upon generations will have better lives because he refused to stop preaching the gospel of Christ."

Luca raised his hands to the empty cross in front of us. "And the greatest of all, Jesus Christ, defeated death. The glory of Jesus doesn't lie in the crucifixion, but in the resurrection. There were thousands of people crucified by the Romans, but nobody knows them. Only Jesus came back to life.

"The greater the mission in life, the greater the price they had to pay."

I said, "My old friend, Daniel, from the Masonic lodge explained to me a few years ago the difference between pain and suffering. I understand now the wisdom in his words. We all have a purpose in life—the function God has given us to fulfill here on earth. In the process, sometimes we suffer, but God gives us the strength to complete our mission. Ignoring our calling, however, brings the unbearable emptiness that everyone seems to have, but nobody talks about. I will finish what I've started."

"I understand your hurt," said Luca. "Let me tell you a story. A few years ago, when you were away with your studies, I hit rock bottom. I was living in the attic of a desolate house with a woman. She despised me. I know because she told me so often. I was a penniless musician, unemployed; she was a young painter, merely a student. Her parents gave us money for food once in a while, but we spent it all on beer and cigarettes. Poverty turned us against each other. We were cursing our lives from the moment we opened our eyes in the morning till we fell asleep, falling-down drunk every evening. We slept on a mattress in a filthy little room with no windows, the two of us and a stray cat we adopted. The place reeked of weed, stale beer, cat food, and cat pee. We had a heater in our room, but the rest of the house was frigid. One night I had to go to the emergency room for dental surgery, and I didn't even have money to pay the doctor. A friend had to come and cover the expenses. I was desperate."

"How did you get out of it?" I asked.

"After he paid for the dentist, my friend took me to his place. I slept at his house. The next morning, he had prepared orange juice and tea for me because I couldn't eat anything, and we talked. I remember the conversation like it was yesterday . . ."

5.

"Haven't you had enough pain? Why do you do this to yourself? You have so much to give, so much to share. You have unique gifts to offer the world."

"What do you mean?" Luca asked. "I'm a loser. I'm dead broke."

"It seems like you've got nothing, but you have more than you are aware of at this very moment of your life. For example, do you remember when we traveled with our friends to Transylvania? That magical evening when you played guitar and shared folk stories and tales of long ago? We loved it. You cooked dinner for us over the campfire in the forest at night, just like the ancients who roamed the mountains thousands of years before us. We were mesmerized by your stories and songs.

"Your passion is music. You spend most of your time reading. You love to tell your friends thrilling ancient tales. Why not offer them to everybody? We would have listened to you all night long. Why not bring the same joy to others? Take your passions—your music and your stories—and transform them into a product: a music album, an unplugged concert, a storytelling evening. What do you have now?"

"I only have a shoddy guitar, old, worn-out, and cracked," Luca protested.

"That's not a problem. That's, in fact, a great asset because your show will be authentic. What seems like a snag to you is in fact a special selling point, if you tell the right story. It will be just like our night in the forest. Your worn-out guitar will take

audiences back to their youth when they camped around the fire in the mountains, when they sang with their friends, smoked holy plants, and were in love with life.

"All you need is a napkin and a pen to make it happen. Here, take the pen from me. Pour your love in this project, and everything else will fall into place with time. Have patience. Don't stop. Write down the songs, talk to people who will help you, ignore all others who won't, and make something magical. Let people see your spirit. After your first performance you will get some money, and it will grow in time, but just do your first show. You have everything you need to get your life back in order."

6.

"I listened to him. Maybe for the first time in my life, I actually listened," Luca told me. "I started working for a music studio. They couldn't pay me, but I slept there on the sofa during the night for more than a year. I discovered a free online archive of myths and legends for my research, and wrote the songs on a yellow notepad. I borrowed an acoustic guitar from somebody for the shows.

"I went from bar to bar and asked the owners if we could organize a storytelling evening together. I kept the money from tickets; they had more customers for the bar. When I had my first live event nine months later, about fifty people showed up, most of them my friends. Then, as the word spread, strangers turned up. On some evenings, I had seventy people—on others, only four. But they loved my work, and this inspired me to keep going.

"I took a job to get me through the year while I was writing new songs. It took five years, and it was hard, but that one idea, written on a napkin with a borrowed pen, gave me a new life."

"I don't know where to turn," I said.

"Your spirit is calling you to empower people to live their dreams, but things didn't turn out as you hoped. You've lost your money, your girl, your friends. You don't know what to do," said Luca. "You trusted your spirit, and you're getting your ass kicked. You're suffering, but in spite of that, your life has meaning, brother. If you keep going, circumstances will change, and you'll come out to light. I promise you!

"Life is never made unbearable by circumstances, but only by lack of purpose. If your work is meaningful, carry on at all cost. I flushed fifteen years of my life away on pleasures and distractions that devastated my mind and body. Drugs, booze, chasing women, chasing shamans, working in advertising, and practicing judo. I've read dozens of books on psychology, discussed philosophy, studied Reiki, and beat the bushes for psychedelic mushrooms. I've done everything except what my spirit was calling me to do: music.

"These distractions took me away from work, and only left me more desolated. I fell into a latent misery that permeated my entire being, a dormant wretchedness that left me empty and barren, and for a good reason: I was not fulfilling my purpose. I had a divine calling, and I refused to do it. What else could I feel but anxiety and fear?

"When people ignore their spirit, they despise life and themselves. I felt unloved for years, not because people didn't love me—I had many friends—but because I had drowned the very part of me that gives life, that feels love, gives love, and is love . . . my heart. For many people, this is the normal way of living, as it has been for me, but this is not life. This is being dead in a body that's still breathing. Don't make the same mistake, my brother."

CHAPTER 15

THE DANGER OF SELF-HELP

When a theory is not working,
something must be wrong with reality.

1.

For seven years, I had holed up in bookstores and read almost everything on the shelves of personal development—from holy books, sacred texts, and ancient manuscripts to business books, entrepreneurship, and leadership how-tos. But, somehow, what I learned in these books didn't prevent me from ending up broke and failing in my work. Trials come regardless of whether you've read about them or not.

What's wrong with me? I wondered. *How can I be so unworthy that I cannot achieve what these books claim everyone can do so fast?* I didn't achieve financial abundance instantly, I didn't make a million dollars in 90 days, the I-don't-know-how-many steps to success didn't lead too far, the secrets turned out to be nothing more than common sense, the three or four or seven things you needed to know were not the only things you must know, and the instant success formulas were deplorable delusions.

So, I began to investigate the scientific literature to find out the truth.

Fact 1: We believe everything we read.

After 400 years of research, scientists discovered that we have a truthfulness bias, a natural tendency to believe what we read, even when it's not true. Every idea, every conversation, every human interaction changes our brain, and others can impose these changes on us against our will. When we receive new information, our brain's instinct is to accept it as true. We have the ability to accept or reject the information, but only after we have initially believed it, and we are not always successful at undoing it.

In an article titled "You Can't Not Believe Everything You Read," Dr. Daniel Gilbert, professor of psychology at Harvard University, wrote: "Acceptance of ideas is passive and inevitable, it happens against our will, whereas rejection of ideas requires mental effort to undo the initial passive acceptance." In other words, we believe *everything*, and then we have to make a conscious choice that requires mental effort to *undo* our belief. To correct our automatic tendency to believe, we have to take a step back and unbelieve. When we're learning something new, and we don't have previous information about the subject, we instantly believe what the others tell us.

Fact 2: We want it all, we want it now, and we can't control it.

We sleep next to our phones, and we wake up in the dead of night to check our texts, e-mails, and updates. We find it ever more difficult to delay gratification, and we want immediate pleasure, or the instant removal of pain. We demand that our lives function like social media: I want it all, and I want it now.

Technology has turned our every wish into an instant demand: on-demand movies, on-demand car rides, on-demand video games, on-demand dating, on-demand life. Dr. Darrell Worthy, professor of psychology at Texas A&M University, discovered that immediate gratification has become the default response when we want something. Waiting is hard, and our unconscious mind has raised immediate gratification to be our main purpose in life. According to a study performed by Common Sense Media, a San Francisco nonprofit that educates families on the safe use of technology, this growing need for instant gratification has robbed us of our most important ability: the ability to think.

Fact 3: Marketers craft the promotional messages to target our emotional response and our uncontrolled want for instant gratification. When products fail to deliver on their promise, we become disillusioned, upset, and disheartened with ourselves (rather than with the product).

We make almost all buying decisions through the filter of our emotions. The impulse to buy a product is triggered by promotional messages that target our emotional responses—our need for love, our need for significance, our fear of loss—and our unconscious demand for instant gratification. Research shows that about 80 percent of the time, impulse purchases lead to financial difficulties, family criticism, guilt, and disappointment.

These three scientific facts—our natural vulnerability to believe everything we read, our uncontrollable demand for instant gratification, and the marketing messages that target our emotional needs and promise a million dollars overnight, instant success, dramatic weight loss, perfect relationships—combine into a dangerous marketing strategy that may backfire against us. We tend to believe that if the instant success formulas don't work, something must be wrong with us, which is the same as saying that if a theory is not working, something must be wrong with reality. Because the brain has already believed the message written in the sales letter, when the product fails to deliver on its promise, and things don't work out the way we expect, we don't challenge the information, but rather we challenge ourselves and our self-worth. Thus something that was created to help, in fact injures us, and we become more disheartened than before.

Regardless of the passing circumstances you find yourself in, your worth is given to you by God—not by other people, not by what you achieve, and not even by yourself. You are as God created you even in the darkest hour. Doing meaningful work takes time, and reality doesn't obey our requests at the snap of a finger.

2.

Years later, my spiritual father shared the following parable with me:

> *Somewhere in a backcountry town in America, an old man found a dollar in the street. He picked it up off the ground and sat down on the sidewalk, holding the ripped bill between his fingers. It was partly caked in mud, worn to shreds, broken.*
>
> *"I wonder what your story is," mused the man.*
>
> *"I've been through a lot," came the answer. "So much has happened to me in all these years. I am very weary and hurt."*
>
> *The old man's gentle eyes grew big in awe, wondering at the voice he heard.*
>
> *"I come from the same place all money comes from," the bill went on. "I was printed one day with millions of other dollar bills, and found myself in this*

world about which I knew nothing. My life began in a little town just like this one. For a while, I brought food to families, toys to children, books and music to the community. Life was good to me, but one day, by mistake, I ended up on a bar top under an empty whiskey glass, then in a back alley in a suitcase. One late night, a man threw me on the nightstand in a dirty motel room, next to an ashtray filled with cigarette butts. A young woman was crying close to me in the dark."

The old man didn't say a word; he just listened.

"One day, a lad crushed me in his fist and threw me on the ground. I've been going with the wind ever since, just as you see me now: broken, shattered, and alone. I don't know where I've gone wrong. I've brought pain to others and hurt people. I didn't mean to do it. Their tears fell on me."

The old man reached in his pocket and pulled out a couple of other bills that looked to be almost new, and gently placed them all together. "I don't know all you've been through," he said softly, "but you have the same worth as any other bill, old or new."

What you've been through in life doesn't change your value. Maybe you underwent many challenges; you might have made choices that hurt you and brought pain to others, suffering greatly when you acted against love. Regardless of what you've done or what you've been through in life, you have the same worth as everybody else. You are equally precious in the eyes of God. You are his son or his daughter, and you are infinitely valuable just the way you are.

CHAPTER 16

CROSSING THE DESERT

Walk ahead, because if you look back, you will go back.

1.

After studying more than 500 successful tech companies, Vivek Wadhwa, director of research at the Center for Entrepreneurship and Research Commercialization at Duke University, concluded that the common belief that young entrepreneurs can turn ideas into billion-dollar companies overnight is nothing more than a myth. The media promotes the few rare outliers, but the reality is very different: the average age of successful entrepreneurs is 40 years old. "Twice as many successful entrepreneurs are over 50 as under 25. The vast majority—75 percent—have more than six years of industry experience, and half have more than ten years when they create their start-up," wrote Wadhwa in *The Washington Post*. Most entrepreneurs are between 55 and 64 years old, and they are twice as likely to build successful start-ups than those between 20 and 35.

Building something that matters is a marathon, not a sprint. Even the rare exceptions must obey the rules of nature. Google started in 1996 as a dissertation project by two students at Stanford University who wanted to explore the mathematical properties of the World Wide Web. The project ran for a year under Stanford University's website at google.stanford.edu, until 1997 when the two students bought their web domain google.com. Yet another year later, they incorporated Google at a friend's garage in Silicon Valley. The founders did 350 pitches to investors before they got funded. Had they stopped along the way, the world today would be totally different.

2.

Worthwhile things take time. Doing the work to transform your dreams into reality is like walking across the earth. It can be that hard, and it can take that long. If you walk from the North Pole to the South Pole, at one point you will go through the desert. It is part of the journey.

When you decide to make your dreams a reality— build that start-up, write that book, release that album, accept that new job offer, move to the new city—you will have to cross the desert. The road darkens somewhere along the way. You don't expect the desert, and you're not prepared for it. When you walk through the shadows, remember the advice of Frank Zappa: "There are only two things to remember. Number one, don't stop, and number two, keep going." You can step in the desert with nothing in your hands, or you might lose it all on the way—but when you're left with nothing, you have nothing to lose.

In the early 1990s, Jack Ma was making $14 a month teaching English at a local university in China. He was rejected from more than 30 jobs before getting his teaching position. Then, in 1995, Jack visited the United States for the first time, and a friend showed him this new thing called the Internet.

When Jack flew home, he crowded 17 friends into his apartment, and they worked around the clock to develop an e-commerce website. Although their company didn't make any money for the first three years, they refused to stop. Finally, after several more years, their idea grew into Alibaba, the biggest online commerce company in the world.

When Alibaba went public, Jack wrote in a letter to his employees: "We haven't survived because our strategies are farsighted and brilliant, or because our execution is perfect, but because for 15 years we have persevered in our mission."

3.

In the desert, you will suffer. You will burn during the day and freeze during the night. This is the way. The desert is part of the passage, there is no other way to get to the other side. Keep going. You will feel afraid, and forsaken by everyone. Your friends might abandon you. They will stay behind, and say you're a fool to walk such a treacherous path. Leave them, just go. Your family will try to stop you because it is not safe to cross the desert. They may be right, but do not listen. Tell them only what they need to know, and carry on in secret if you must.

In the 1960s, Paulo, a troubled teenager from Brazil, told his parents that he wanted to become a writer. However, his parents opposed the idea and committed him to a mental institution. He escaped from the sanatorium, and found refuge in drugs, sex, and the hippie lifestyle of the time. He gave up his dream of being a writer, and undertook shadow careers working as a journalist or writing song lyrics to make a living.

He picked up the pen again when he was 35, but his first book failed. Five years later, he published another novel through a small Brazilian publisher. They printed only 900 copies, and then stopped because it wasn't selling. So Paulo knocked on doors and asked others to publish the book again, even though it had flopped before. Another company bought the rights and published it six years later under the name *The Alchemist*.

Paulo Coelho's novel took off and became one of the best-selling books of all times, translated into 80 languages, and even holding the Guinness World Record for the "most translated book by a living author." His journey through the desert was difficult, and it took more than 30 years.

How was he able to keep going? As Paulo explained to Oprah Winfrey, "There is a sentence in the book that says: *When you want something, the whole universe conspires to help you.* I wrote this. I have to live by these words."

4.

Driven by a desire to become a missionary, Mother Teresa left her family in Albania at the age of 18 to join the Sisters of Loreto in Ireland. Before she left home, her mom gave her a piece of wisdom that remained with Teresa her entire life. Her mom's words became the light in her moments of doubt: "Put your hand in [Jesus's] hand, and walk alone with him. Walk ahead, because if you look back, you will go back."

In the desert, you will doubt yourself and mistrust the world. You will feel ashamed to share your suffering with others. You will curse. You will raise your hands to the sky. You will blame God. You will kneel, cry, crush your head in your palms, and beg for a sign. It will not come. Nobody will answer. The desert has no mercy on you. Whatever you do, do not look behind you, because if you look back, you go back.

You will be angry at others who seem to have easier lives. They do. They never dared to cross the desert. You will seem to be in danger, but you are actually living. They will seem to be safe, but they are actually dying.

"Life ends for most people, who stiffen in the attitudes they adopt to make themselves suitable for the jobs and lives that other people have laid out for them," as V. S. Naipaul wrote. You will not know this. You will believe circumstances define you, and you will think you're a failure. When you get discouraged, that's just the devil doing his work. "Keep your mind in hell, and do not despair," as Father Silouan, a monk from Mount Athos in Greece, said. Remain in Truth, and do the work. Don't stop for anything, because your next step could be the one out into the light.

In the 1980s, a kid from New Jersey formed a rock band and played evenings in bars. During the day, he sold newspaper subscriptions door to door and worked in a junkyard, a car wash, and a fast-food restaurant. He later got a job to sweep the floor, make coffee, bring snacks to clients, and run errands for a music studio. With the money he earned, he recorded his demo songs during the night, when the studio was a lot cheaper.

One evening he went to a local radio station. They didn't have a receptionist, so he walked in and gave the tape to the DJ. They aired the song, and eventually other radio stations in New York picked up the tune. When this first song aired on the radio, the kid had recorded over 400 songs—that's about 40 albums nobody ever heard. After 10 years of running on faith and working without a reward, with record labels rejecting him and dismissing his music, this kid became Jon Bon Jovi, one of the most loved musicians of all time.

5.

When you feel abandoned, look above you. The stars you see in your darkest hour are little cracks in the floor of heaven, through which the divine light shines.

You are never alone. When your will is aligned with the divine will, you can dream, imagine, learn, do, suffer, fail, curse, get up, and keep going. The moment you begin lying to yourself, you're done. You fall back into pain, and you're on your way to the grave. Don't believe everything you think, and don't obey everything you feel.

From time to time, you will try to turn back. You will believe you have made a terrible mistake. You will demand God to tell you what you have done to deserve such suffering. No answer will come. You will blame yourself. You will want to give up, and you will feel lost in the middle of nowhere. You have ventured off into the great unknown, and the desert is trying its best to bury you. When you begin telling yourself that you are not worthy, that you don't deserve anything, you will know that the desert is winning its game.

Write in your heart, and live the words of the Indian poet Rabindranath Tagore: "Let me not pray to be sheltered from dangers but to be fearless in facing them. Let me not beg for the stilling of my pain, but for the heart to conquer it." The question you must answer is this: Are you willing to cross the desert? Because, in the end, only the traveler gets to tell the story. The rest have no stories to tell. The crowd remains wondering, "What if?"

You cannot talk about grit. You have to embody it.

You cannot talk about faith. You have to live it.

You cannot talk about the desert. You have to cross it.

6.

Faith is the bridge over the gap you have chosen. Most of us, at one point or another, say, "If I only had more faith, I would follow my dream." Faith is the cornerstone of our dreams, but is also very misunderstood. Faith is not belief. Faith cannot be fabricated by repetitions or affirmations, or manufactured by mental techniques. Faith is God's gift planted in our heart in the form of a seed.

The seed of a tree is the *substance* (you can observe it) and *evidence* of the tree that will come in the future when the process of growth is complete. The seed must be put in the ground, where the tree will grow in time. In a similar way, faith is the *seed* of your dream fulfilled. When God puts the seed of faith in your heart, faith becomes the *substance* (you can observe it) and the *evidence* of your dream becoming reality in the future when the work is complete. You don't need more faith than a mustard seed.

Meaningful things in life take time, and crossing the desert requires patience. Patience is the child of faith; if you have faith, you will do anything it takes, for as long as it takes, to make your dream a reality. Faith is born out of love, and love *never* fails. Therefore, don't ask for more faith—just love more. Work to make your heart pure. It all starts by living in Truth.

When people walk in faith, the crowd perceives arrogance. Faith means you dare to cross the desert, even if you must do it alone. You do the work regardless of what the crowd says. People who dare to cross the desert, and make their dreams a reality, are not special people. They are ordinary people who live in Truth, because they know there's no other way to live. They are common people who do everyday things, and create a destiny for themselves even when the world doesn't care. They are ignored, misunderstood, or looked right through by the crowd. They are humble, look meek, and nobody notices their value, but they carry on in faith until the day when their suffering turns into greatness. They cross the desert of their dreams, face the dark night alone, defeat resistance, and work until they have a breakthrough. They do work that matters, even when nobody is watching. They knock down barrier after barrier because they know that if they refuse to stop, the Universe will give in.

CHAPTER 17

HALLELUJAH

*Our acts of love have effects far beyond
our awareness of them.*

March 2014. Bucharest.

1.

I met my team in an Irish pub in Bucharest. The blizzard formed a cheerful dance of snowflakes under the yellow streetlights, over the music of cars whooshing through the slush. Outside the pub, a bike, two empty tables covered in snow, and I were waiting for a change of seasons. Gazing through the window, I could see my friends already inside.

Walking in, all around me were only shapes and shadows, moving through the cigarette-smoke cloud. I approached my friends and told them that I had made a decision. A year had passed since we'd filmed the interviews for the film, and nothing had changed. This project meant nothing to them, but everything to me. We began together, but I was going to finish alone.

I was worried about their reaction, but they agreed or just didn't care. They all wished me luck, and reminded me once again that I was still a nobody, and that my presence would desecrate the film.

I walked out again in snow but also in freedom.

2.

I made a list of everything I still needed: videos to illustrate the story, music to give rhythm, an editor to put all the pieces of the narrative together, and an audio engineer for the soundtrack. I was still broke, so paying for these was out of the question.

Somebody recommended that I do a crowdfunding campaign: if people contributed to my idea, I could use the money to buy videos and music, and commission a team for the film. But after all, money is just a means to an end, not the final goal. So I decided to jump the means, and go straight to the end. I didn't need money; I needed *videos and music*.

I wrote to more than 30 filmmakers—all throughout North America, South America, Europe, Australia, New Zealand—and asked if they would like to contribute to my movie with their best work. Most said yes.

I wrote to music companies and asked them to sponsor the film, not with money but with songs. Most said no. After a few more weeks of research, a friend of a friend who owned a music-publishing business offered me the songs as a gift.

When you follow your dreams, you will think you need money. What do you need the money for? Go straight for what you actually need.

As for the editing, I did that myself. I spent three months in front of my laptop from morning to midnight. I learned the software, watched the interviews, listened to hours of music, wrote the story. I ate hummus and cucumber sandwiches on my keyboard, brushed my teeth with one hand and worked with the other, put all the pieces of the puzzle together, talked to nobody—and just did the work.

A friend from college who was just building his recording studio agreed to work with me on the soundtrack. One late night, I got out of the metro in an industrial part of the city and walked straight into a blizzard. My feet slid, one forward and one backward, or perhaps both went sideways; I was wearing banana peels, not sneakers. I clung to my hat with one hand and tried to find my balance with the other, above all attempting not to fall on my back and crack my laptop.

I finally found my friend at his studio in an old deserted mill. There was no elevator and no light. We climbed the stairs while clinging to the walls. The first floor had not been used for years, and snow piled up inside next to the broken windows. He opened the door to the studio, revealing a single lamp underneath a desk. An old jazz guitar lay on the floor, together with miles of cables coiled and crawling like snakes. There was a keyboard and many plastic cups half-filled with whiskey, coffee, and cigarette butts.

We turned sound into white clouds when we talked. I sat on a chair in the dark, and he worked on the computer with his gloves on, standing and bouncing twice on one leg, twice on the other. The dankness made the room colder than outside. We jumped, we laughed, we chattered, we shook, and we got the work done.

Finally, the movie was finished.

3.

The night before the official release, I woke up at 3 A.M., shivering in bed. My heart was aching, and I could see its pounding through my thin T-shirt. *What if nobody likes the movie? What will people say? What if the movie is a failure?* A deluge of thoughts rushed through my mind. The voices were back.

My clothes were wet, and my face dripped with sweat. *What if my friends were right, and I really shouldn't be in the film? What if the celebrities in the movie think the same?* The demons of the past took over my mind and unleashed a panic attack. The room was spinning around me. An hour later, I was exhausted from fear.

I did my best. I gave this project everything I had. If it's not enough for others, then there's nothing I can do. In my heart of hearts I knew I had created this project with the best intentions. *I had given it my best.*

I released the film the following day.

4.

My demons' words never manifested into reality. I worked on *The Amazing You* for more than a year, hoping it would help people make their dreams a reality, but I never imagined that its impact could be so profound. People from all over the world, from all walks of life, began writing to me.

A man from New York, who had just turned 75, sent me a letter saying that he hasn't lived since his wife died 15 years before, but after seeing the movie, he's come back to life. A woman from New Zealand wrote me that her husband had committed suicide in their house only days before, and left her alone with their seven-year-old son. She didn't know what to do, but after she watched the film, she had found the strength to carry on.

When I read these letters, I realized that all the suffering I'd been through had been worthwhile, if only for helping a handful of people get through those dark moments. Parents on all continents said that the film should be included in all high schools and universities. A teacher from Syria wrote me to say that the movie could change the lives of students after the painful years of war.

People wrote from all corners of the world to say that my movie had given them healing, hope, inspiration, and the power to live again. I received offers from volunteers to translate the movie so that it could be offered in their country. Eventually, it became available in 20 languages.

The film took me on an extraordinary journey around the world, and it opened doors I never imagined existed. If I told you the stories, I would fill another book with the adventures I've been on and the miracles I've seen—and it all started from making this movie.

I discovered that, in spite of the suffering we sometimes go through to fulfill our dreams, our acts of love have effects far beyond our awareness of them. Not even in my wildest fantasies did I imagine that in two years, the lives of people in 56 countries could be touched by a broke student from Romania, slipping in sneakers in the snow.

CHAPTER 18

THE GOSPEL OF RAY

*Failure is cheaper than ever before,
and there's no reason to fear anymore.*

1.

Singularity University was founded by Peter Diamandis, an entrepreneur on a mission to open space travel for everyone, and Ray Kurzweil, Google's director of engineering. Ray, whom PBS named as one of 16 "revolutionaries who made America," holds 21 honorary doctorates for his innovations in many fields, including artificial intelligence.

Ray doesn't look into a crystal ball, but he has predicted the future with astonishing accuracy using advanced mathematical models. In his book written in the 1990s, *The Age of Spiritual Machines*, Ray made 147 predictions about how technology would change the world in the following decades; 86 percent of them turned out correct, while another 12 percent were deemed "partially correct."

Among his many predictions, Ray foresaw the rise of portable and wearable personal computers and devices that "make phone calls, access the Web, monitor body functions, provide directions, and provide a variety of other services." He predicted that computers would include wireless technology to plug into the ever-present worldwide network. Today, any child connecting their smartphone to Wi-Fi would agree that Ray was exceptionally accurate. Scientists, experts, and the general public regarded Ray and his predictions as insane each time he made them, but perfectly normal when they came true.

Five hundred years ago, the world stayed the same for decades. Children lived the way their grandparents lived, and nobody expected things to change. Today's children live in a world that didn't exist for their parents. There is a saying that the only constant is change, but this idea is not true anymore. Change is getting faster and faster when it comes to information technology, because we are using faster computers to build faster computers, and we are faster at building them each year. Change is accelerating.

Ray came to MIT in 1965 as a student because MIT was so advanced that it actually had its own computer. It occupied half a building, cost about $11 million, and was shared by thousands of students. In the 1960s, computers were so big that they were transported by forklift. Today, a computer fits into your mobile phone, and everybody has one because they are extremely cheap. The smartphones in our pockets are thousands of times faster and more powerful than the computers NASA used to send astronauts to the moon during the Apollo missions.

We have been technologically advanced for only a century or so, and we have been using digital technologies for just a few decades. According to Peter Diamandis, we live in the stone age of technology, and the future will bring an extraordinary progress. Ray forecasts that in 2029, the intelligence of computers will transcend the intelligence of the human brain, and we will not be able to keep up with our inventions unless we enhance our own brains by merging them with the very technologies we are now developing. In 2030 we will have millions of robots the size of our cells cruising through our bodies to enhance our health. We will send these nanorobots to our brains, connect them with our neurons, and then these nanorobots will boost our brainpower and link us to the Internet. In the same way that cars extend our physical ability to travel faster and farther, nanorobots connected to our brain will extend our ability to think.

By 2040 the artificial intelligence will be smarter than all human brains combined, and by 2050 we will upload our minds to computers, or transfer our minds to robots that will replace our bodies.

2.

Technology is unleashing an abundance of opportunities for all, regardless of where we are on earth. In spite of the evidence, there's still a giant chasm between the scientific reality and the way media presents our world. If you open any newspaper, or turn to any news channel, the world looks bleak and seems to be getting worse. Ray and his fellow researchers at Singularity University show that the world is far better than we think, and it is only getting better. The media is not science, and they have an important reason to paint a false, very grim picture of reality.

More than 90 percent of the daily news is negative: increasing problems about population size, financial crises, corruption, water and food scarcity, health threats and pandemics, social unrest and conflicts, terrorism, war, and natural disasters. The news media has a preference to feed us negative news and constant dangers in high-definition. No wonder we are fearful about our lives, about other people, about the world, and about the future.

The goal of the media is to sell our eyes to advertisers. That's how they make their money. The more we are hooked to their channels, the more money they make. The reason why we see mostly negative news is because, to keep our attention locked, they feed off our biological weakness for fear and target one of the most ancient responses of our brain to danger.

Every second of every day, an infinite amount of data from the environment floods our brain through our five senses. Our conscious mind can only process a very tiny fragment of that information, and the rest is evaluated by the brain in an unconscious, automatic manner. The brain filters the incoming data, and sorts out what is critical from what is insignificant. Its top priority and concern—far more important than everything else—is survival. Considering the flood of negative news, we live in a constant state of fear, angst, and worry. Our brains have evolved to be exceedingly aware of all possible dangers in the environment, but this adaptation came with the cost of shutting down our ability to accept good news.

3.

There are still many problems that we must solve, but science shows that the world is actually far better than we think. Research at Singularity University reveals that we are living during the most peaceful times in history, with violence and conflicts at all-time lows. In the last 100 years, child and maternal mortality decreased by more than 90 percent, and the average human life span more than doubled. In 2013, *TIME* magazine and *National Geographic* reported that the babies who will live 120 years have already been born.

We will soon have the ability to meet the needs of every human on our planet and provide everyone with goods and services that were once reserved only for the rich. In just 20 years, between 1990 and 2010, more than one billion people in developing countries have risen out of poverty. Poverty has declined more in the past 50 years than in the last 500 years, and studies show that we will end global poverty by the end of 2030. Every decade we redefine what poverty means: 99 percent of people who live under the poverty line in developed countries have electricity, water, refrigerators, and a flush toilet; 95 percent have a TV; 88 percent have a mobile phone; and 70 percent have a car and air-conditioning. Not even the kings, the queens, and the richest people of the world dreamed of such luxuries a hundred years ago. "Abundance is not about providing everyone on this planet with a life of luxury—rather it's about providing all with a life of possibility," wrote Peter Diamandis in his book *Abundance*. We are creating, he says, "a world where everyone's days are spent dreaming and doing, not scrapping and scraping."

Education is open to everyone, anywhere in the world, as various educational materials and courses from top universities are now available free online and can be accessed on every smartphone connected to the Internet. Recently, Peter Diamandis talked about the promise of the "rising billions": the three to five billion people who will connect to the Internet for the first time by 2020, learning, spending money, making their voices heard, and bringing their ideas, products, and demands to the emerging global market.

"Technology is a resource-liberating force," wrote Diamandis. We are set free from the everyday struggles of meeting our basic needs, and we can now focus on our life's purpose, on our dreams, and the contribution we want to make in the world. A global movement of do-it-yourselfers began in the 1950s, and keeps growing. Individuals with ideas, driven by a sense of purpose, are facing humanity's grandest challenges and changing the world. Innovators and entrepreneurs are solving problems that were once tackled only by governments and major corporations, including major breakthroughs in medicine, bringing clean water to poverty-stricken countries, and even building commercial spacecraft. The cost of launching an Internet start-up has dropped from $5 million in the 1990s to a few thousand dollars today; one can even start an online business with *zero* money.

Failure is cheaper than ever before, and there's no reason to fear anymore. The data show that this progress has continued through good times and bad, through war and peace, and our lives will continue to improve regardless of the sensations in the news.

July 2015. Silicon Valley, California.

4.

One evening, after the lights had been turned off at the NASA center in Silicon Valley where Singularity University is located, my colleagues and I sat on beanbags in a circle in the classroom, chatting about Ray's predictions. Rebecca, one of Google's leading innovators, grabbed a Coke and joined our conversation.

"What do you think now that you've seen the real data?" she asked.

"Humanity has been through enough suffering, and everyone has the opportunity to make a positive impact, if they decide to do so," someone piped up.

"In my travels around the world," I said, "I asked people what they would do with their life if money didn't matter—what ignites the spark within them, what makes them so passionate and alive that they would wake up before dawn every day for ten years to do the work—and they all said the same thing: they want to do something meaningful, to help others."

"There is nothing we cannot do today," said Rebecca. "No matter who you are, if you have the passion, the drive, and the grit, you can make your dreams a reality anywhere you start, and become successful in the process of doing good in the world. But we must change our focus from blaming and complaining about our problems, to working and solving our problems. We must become so absorbed with our dreams that we don't have a spare moment to look at what others are doing."

I said, "A single entrepreneur, a single artist, a single start-up, or a single company cannot change the world, but nine hundred million of us can. What if I told you that according to research, there are nine hundred million people in the world who have jobs, education, skills, but who are miserable and don't care about what they do? They go to work every day, but don't give a damn.

"Young people are the most unfulfilled, and bother least about what they do. They value their freedom and their creativity, living their passion and doing meaningful work, more than having a secure job and a good salary. Can you imagine the impact these people can have in the world if they did something they cared for?"

"The educational system has been developed to train us and to position us so that we find a job," Rebecca said. "Not to give us freedom, not to give us a sense of purpose, not to give us a life. To give us a job. We grow up in a culture where we are taught to be of value to somebody else's vision, and get a job. And this system is now failing.

Google's futurist Thomas Frey predicts that half of the jobs will be automated in the next decade."

"What will people do then?" someone asked.

"The only way to thrive in the future is to focus on what you love, develop knowledge and skills in the service of your passion, and be relentless in doing the work," said Rebecca.

"There are many successful entrepreneurs in Silicon Valley because they fail so much more than everyone else," I said. "The social context in the valley empowers people to create leading-edge products and companies, because everyone understands that it's okay to fail."

Rebecca continued. "Entrepreneurs have a rule: *Do. Think. Do.* We first *do*, then we *think* about what we've done, then we learn and *do it better* next time. This happens fast because we need to learn, and we learn only by doing. Failure is nothing more than doing and learning, but doing always precedes understanding. The people who are unfulfilled in their jobs could live their passion now, but they don't because they are still thinking. They have to start doing."

"Working on your passion, and building something meaningful can be much harder than the path of having a job, but it's the only way to create your future, and the only worthwhile way to live your life," I said. "When you transform your idea into reality, when the seed becomes the tree in blossom, when you walk out of the desert and into the light, you forget all the days, the weeks, the months, and the years of endless torment, frustrations, and stress. You forget all the rejections you got along the way. We invent our own future, but we must pay the price."

"Thinking about the future is the worst way of thinking about the future. Working on your future is the best way of thinking about your future. You learn only by doing, but herein lies the problem," said Rebecca. "Let's say you're in a job. You want to make a change in your life. What do you do?"

"You get another job," someone said, and we all laughed.

"Exactly. You know why?" asked Rebecca in a serious tone. "Doing always *precedes* knowing. You do what you know, and you only know what you have done before. Because you had a job for years, you know how to do that. Because you never had your own start-up, you don't know how to do that. Doing what you don't know brings fear and uncertainty. Your brain thinks fear is danger—which, by the way, are two different things because you can be afraid for no reason, and you can be in danger without knowing it—and prevents you from stepping into the unknown. You then go about doing what you know, because the known gives you a sense of security. So you find another job, and begin the process all over again. You drag the past into the future. If you want to create a different future, you have to do what you haven't done before. You must walk into the unknown."

"In the end, it all comes down to accepting the uncomfortable reality about your life. Is what you are now doing—not *thinking* of doing, but *actually* doing—taking you to a future you want to live in, or not? Are you, in fact, doing what you know in your heart you must do?" someone else said.

"People will probably think that Ray's predictions for the future are nothing more than the delusions of a man without the fear of God," said Rebecca. "Some people are thrilled about his predictions; some are terrified by them. It doesn't really matter if Ray is right or wrong about the future. The reality is that the world of 1950 is not the world of 2000.

"Flip this forward to 2050. What will the world look like then? We don't know. Telamon of Arcadia, a Greek mercenary from the fifth century B.C., said 'It is one thing to study war, and another to live a warrior's life.' If you want to create your future, you must stop thinking, and start doing. If you are not relentless in doing the work, you will find yourself living in someone else's future, and you will not have a word to say about it."

5.

The summer I spent at Singularity University opened my eyes to the abundant world we live in today. If you do the research, you will find a wealth of opportunities available for your life. Only two things will keep you from living your dreams: not knowing that the opportunities are out there, and not having the willingness to work hard to find them or make them. If you are willing to study and do the work long-term, nothing will stop you from fulfilling your dreams.

The continuous cycle of learning and working breathes new life into broken dreams, and brings fresh hope to broken hearts. The world is better than you think, and the social environment today empowers you to follow your dreams—but you *must* do the work.

CHAPTER 19

THE MEANING OF LIFE

I never understood why a scientist can't pray,
and why a spiritual person can't think.

July 2014. Greece.

1.

A few months after I released the film, I took a break from everything and went on holiday, still trying to heal and pick up the pieces of my life. My new girlfriend and I got off the ferry on the little Greek island of Samothrace when the sun just dragged itself from the sheets below the water and above the horizon. The final slice of the moon disappeared from the pink sky. Fishermen left the harbor and drifted with their boats to the open sea. I drove our little car on the only road that goes around the island, with the waves on our left and the forest on our right. My girl's body was pressed up against the door, practically hanging out the window, her hair flowing in the wind. I held the wheel with one hand, and caressed her leg with the other. She clung with one hand to the car roof, smiling and singing rock-and-roll lyrics to passersby.

The biblical Garden of Eden was inspired by this little island floating in the Aegean Sea. The main road was filled with shirtless men zooming by on scooters, pickup trucks with happy dogs barking from the beds. Keep driving and in one hour, you'll find yourself back where you started.

We parked the car in front of the fishermen's restaurant with tables scattered on the beach and walked in the opposite direction into the forest. We hiked on the bank of the river close to ancient cliff walls, and we climbed the mountain along waterfalls that crashed down from the clouds. From place to place, the river slowed down and formed ponds. Young women wearing only prayer beads, and some a feather necklace, sat on the warm rocks. They played instruments and drummed to the music of the river. They jumped and screamed and laughed when they splashed in the water. When I jumped in, my lips turned blue from the cold. I used all my energy to just breathe and get out.

I stretched out on a sun-bathed rock and played my flute, while the ladies kept drumming with their eyes closed and heads tilted back. The forest smelled of cold river, pine trees, flowers, and sun-drenched skin.

We hiked for hours on a dirt road under the Greek sun before we reached the monastery on top of the mountain. We put our backpacks down on a wooden bench in front of the monastic cell, and sat down on the stairs. Monks painted white this Orthodox cell, with humble and minimalist beauty. A little blue cross above the door looked like a pendant around the neck of a woman saint. Wind made the old bell that swung from a solitary tree behind us clang. The tree grew out of the rocks and overlooked the abyss below.

The legend says that the early inhabitants of the island lived down in the valley, and they built their church in the center of the village. When barbarians attacked them, the monks took the icon of Virgin Mary from the altar and threw it into the sea to prevent it from falling into the hands of thieves. Several hundred years later, a ship was sailing the Greek seas when a storm broke out. The captain saw the icon floating on the waves and pulled it onto the deck. The storm ceased immediately. Mary the Blessed Virgin appeared to the captain in a dream that night and told him to take the icon to the island of Samothrace. They docked in the harbor a few days later. The captain put the icon back in the church, but it disappeared again from the altar. Locals found it on top of the mountain. They built this monastic cell, Madonna of the Cliffs, on the rock where they found the icon, to overlook the island and the sea from above the clouds.

Nobody else was in the garden, and we took turns going in the monastery. I closed the little white door, sat down on a stone-carved armchair, closed my eyes, and prayed:

> *"Father, I do not know you, but I want to. Some people say I have sins that will never be forgiven. Some say I cannot come before you as dirty as I am. Some say you don't even exist. Here's what I say:*
>
> *"You know my past. You know my mistakes. You know my fears and my hurt. I do not know your plans for me. I cannot change the past and everything I've done wrong. When the time comes, you decide what you do with me because you hold the power over all things.*
>
> *"However, Father, there is one thing that is not in your power to do, but in mine. The choice for me to love you is not yours. The choice for me to love you with all my heart and soul is mine. From today and in every moment, I come to you just as I am, naked, broken, hurt, and lost, to give you my love.*

"With nothing in my hands to give you, I come to you to give you my heart. To give you my love. I stand before you, Father, not to ask and take, but to love you more each day.

"I ask for nothing, but just to do your will. I surrender my body, my mind, my heart, and my life to you.

"I am grateful for your gifts, but today I seek not the gifts, but you—the giver of all gifts. I love not what you give me, but you—the one who's always given to me. In all humility and reverence, I thank you for my life, Father. I thank you for your sweet son Jesus, for without him we would still be slogging through the darkness, but with him we can move mountains. I thank you for the Holy Spirit, the precious giver of all inspiration, healing, power, and peace.

"Just as I am, open, honest, in spirit, and in truth,
"I love you, Father."

2.

My girl and I walked outside the garden, holding hands, but after a few steps we stood still. Night had fallen over the mountain. I could tell my eyes were open because I saw a few stars twinkling above us, but when I looked around it was as dark as if my eyes were closed. I stretched out my hand to pick a star, and I would have probably reached it if I had just jumped a little. The fragment of the moon above quivered like a silver comma in the sea below us.

The crickets, our footsteps shuffling in the dirt, and the goats jingling their bells in the valley brought music to the stillness of the night. The clinking of glasses, knives, and forks on plates, voices, and laughter filled in the song from a house somewhere close. I put my hands on the edge of the fence, and pulled myself to look in the garden, where the voices were coming from.

"*Kalispera!*" said a man from the table. The shadow of his hand waved through the air. "Join us!"

"Good evening," I said to the silhouettes sitting around the table. Another shadow figure moved toward us. A man dressed in black, with glasses and a white beard, opened the gate. A traditional Christian Orthodox pendant—the silver cross with three horizontal crossbeams—around his neck glittered in the moonlight.

"I can't see anything," I whispered, as we followed the sound of his footsteps on the crushed stone in the garden.

"To those who wish to see, God gives sufficient light. To those who do not wish to see, he gives sufficient darkness." The old man spoke in English with a thick Greek accent. "Sit down."

"I hope you enjoyed our humble church," said a woman who was fussing with a baby in a stroller at the head of the table. "We saw you when you walked in hours ago. My father takes care of it. He didn't mean to scare you." The flickering candles on the table caused shadows to dance across her face as she shook my hand. "I'm Penelope."

"This place has a kind of holiness," I said. "Thank you for welcoming us into your home."

"Father Alexios was born on this island, down in the harbor town," said the man sitting next to Penelope. "He came up here on the mountain when he was sixteen and never left. He is now seventy and still serves God with all his heart." The man took Penelope's hand, which was resting on the table next to a plate. "Father Alexios married us a few years ago and baptized our little Theodor," he said, gesturing to the baby.

"We live on the mainland in Greece, two hours by ferry from the island," said Penelope. "We come here once a month to see my father and attend his service. You are both welcome this Sunday, if you want to join us."

I replied. "Years ago I thought about becoming a monk in a monastery in Romania, but I realized it wasn't for me. I am still looking for God—in my prayers, in other people, in myself, in my pilgrimages around the world. I am still trying to find meaning and the 'peace that passeth all understanding.'"

"We all are. The meaning of life lies hidden in searching for the meaning of life," said Father Alexios. "Whoever seeks will find, and the finding will cause him to seek even more, but in seeking lies hidden the meaning of life."

"I am still learning, still seeking," I said.

"Meaning can be found only in searching for Truth, and living with the Truth. You will be troubled at first by the contemplation of the Truth, but once you've lived through your anguish, you stand in awe at the peace that you find on the other side of fear," he said. "It is not easy to open your heart, because the path to Truth takes you through the depths of torment. Those who want to find life pass first through the valley of fear."

Father Alexios took a piece of steaming bread and dipped it in tzatziki sauce. "Just as a mother feeds her baby with milk from her breast and love from her heart, in the same way God feeds us with bread from the earth and love from his spirit," he said. "We all receive God's gifts, but we don't appreciate them alike. Living your life on purpose means living your live in obedience to God."

Penelope spoke up. "A thousand teachers and a thousand schools teach a thousand truths, but the reality is simple: God is love, and when we love, we become the living expression of holiness. Our lips of clay speak words of healing; our hands lift people up. We show mercy, and we bring hope. Do you know that all we have to do to fill the emptiness within is to be sincere in our search for God and make our hearts pure? The greatest ailment people suffer from can be healed in such an effortless way: open your heart and seek God with all honesty. When we don't live with God, we become a hollow shell, fragile and easily breakable. When you surrender to God every day, your entire life begins to heal and have meaning."

Father Alexios nodded, then glanced at the candles burning on the table. The smell of grapes and flowers and night chill filled the air. We remained silent for a while to listen to the goats bleating in the valley.

3.

"There are three voices you hear all the time," said Father Alexios. "The body, the mind, and the spirit—they all speak to you. You can obey, even become enslaved by the cravings of the body; ask any person struggling with addiction. You can chase the ghosts of the mind: personal agendas, fretting about what others think of you, wanting to be like others. Or you can listen to the voice of spirit and be free. The spirit of God lives in you, and the spirit always tells you the truth, because the spirit *is* the Truth. What voice do you choose to listen to? That's the real question.

"People travel to this little church from far away to tell me they've been praying and praying, and nothing has happened. Do you know you don't receive anything until you ask God in spirit and in truth? Don't ask from your mind or from your emotions, because thoughts and feelings don't have life unless your spirit breathes life into them. When you pray, ask from your heart and you will be answered.

"The secret to life," continued Father Alexios, looking me straight in the eyes, "is to put the power of creation, which is our mind"—with this, he touched his forehead with his fingers—"in the service of spirit, in the service of love." He put his right hand on his heart. "To develop our mind, and make it the servant of love. The journey in life must be taken with the body, the mind, and the heart together, but it is the spirit that speaks for the Truth.

"For example," Father Alexios continued, taking his daughter's hand, "Penelope, you love this baby. You feel in your heart that you love him beyond this world. You think of him in every moment, and you learn all that you can to be a good mother. You do everything for this child."

"She does," said her husband. "This baby is our life."

"Love came first, thinking and doing followed. But when it comes to our own lives, most of us stumble and fall," Father Alexios said. "Our heart calls us one way, the mind pulls us the other way, and we don't do much. We cannot find peace when the mind wages war against the heart, when we fight with our thoughts the pull of our love. This inner conflict tears us apart."

Penelope took Theodor from the stroller and embraced him.

"The mind and the body are servants of spirit. The body without wisdom and love is like an abandoned house left into ruin, and darkness abounds inside. The mind without a body to live in, and without a heart to feel, is like a book with dead pages. The heart without wisdom to create from love, and without a body to do the work, burns to its own destruction," said Father Alexios.

"Do you know that the way in which God created the universe is the same way for us to fulfill our destiny? *The story of creation is actually the secret to creating*," he continued. "God is love, and love was first. Before anything was made, God created Wisdom. Wisdom is the child of Love, the first of all creations. Together, Love and Wisdom brought forth all things, and through their work the Heavens and the Earth were made.

"In Genesis 1:26, God said, 'Let us make man in our image, after our likeness.' He wasn't referring to himself as *we*, or taking to and by himself. He was talking to Wisdom (Proverbs 8:22–31). Love and Wisdom then got their hands dirty and made us in their likeness: to be love and to have wisdom.

"We create in the same way in life: we discover the love in our hearts. Our love then gives birth to wisdom, and we work to make things happen. The work brings forth more wisdom, which in turn unveils new ideas for new work, and thus creation expands forever. Everything begins with love, and everything is created *through* work."

"I worked in aerospace for many years," I said. "Nobody talked about their feelings or about their hearts."

Father Alexios continued. "Hundreds of years ago people looked to the sky and dreamed about flying. Their hearts burned with enthusiasm, but they didn't have the knowledge of how to fly. They put wings on their backs and flapped them off a building, or fastened them to a bike, jumped off a cliff, and died. They had passion, but no wisdom.

"Today people are driven by the same enthusiasm for flying. The same love burns in their hearts as it did hundreds of years ago, but they also developed understanding. They have passion and knowledge. When mind and heart joined as one, we flew across the earth. If people didn't have enthusiasm, they would never have persisted in risking their lives. If they hadn't developed knowledge, they would have gone on killing themselves. Passion without wisdom destroys itself, and wisdom without passion throws us into the most barren existence. If you want to truly live, you must align your thoughts, your feelings, and your actions."

I replied, "We can see the value of science in the world. Technology has transformed our lives. We are healthy. We live longer. We travel. We communicate with each other from the other side of the planet. I never understood, however, why a scientist can't pray, and why a spiritual person can't think. We have this tendency to separate science and spirituality, as if we must choose just one path. If we embrace both, we have more knowledge than they hold by themselves. We understand more than science can understand by itself, and more than the spiritual traditions can ever know by themselves."

"Maximus the Confessor answered your question in the year 600. True knowledge is received with the body, the mind, and the spirit together. Any fragmentation of these is a fragmentation of the truth," said Father Alexios.

"Give the keys to your life to God, not to other people," said Penelope. "Close your eyes to the world, and look only within yourself because only within yourself can you know the Truth of who you are."

"First," said Father Alexios, raising one finger, "you must listen to the voice of spirit in your heart. Don't ignore it anymore."

He raised a second finger. "Second, you must put your mind in the service of your heart. Grow in wisdom, and develop knowledge that empowers you to live in and with the Truth. The mind must become an instrument to serve love. Jesus said, 'Be wise as serpents and innocent as doves' (Matthew 10:16). In other words, keep your heart untainted by evil, and don't be stupid. Learn every day, grow in wisdom."

He raised one more finger. "Third, remember these words of Jesus: 'Everyone who comes to me, and hears my words, and does them, I will show you who he is like. He is like a man building a house, who dug and went deep, and laid a foundation on the rock. When a flood arose, the stream broke against that house, and could not shake it, because it was founded on the rock. But he who hears, and doesn't do, is like a man who built a house on the earth without a foundation, against which the stream broke, and immediately it fell, and the ruin of that house was great (Luke 6:47–49).'

"Your life is the fruit of what you do. All the knowledge in the world means nothing if you don't live the teachings. You matter, whether you know it or not, and you are here on earth for a purpose, but you can fulfill your destiny only by doing the work. Your persistent actions are the bridge between mind and matter, between the inner and the outer. Do what you've been called to do. Do it with grit, do it with courage, do it with boldness and faith, and do it every day for the rest of your life."

CHAPTER 20

CONNECTING SCIENCE, MEANING, LOVE, AND THE IMPOSSIBLE

The best moments of our lives are those when we reach beyond ourselves, live with meaning, and go into the unknown with an open heart.

1.

In the 1970s, Dr. Mihaly Csikszentmihalyi, professor of psychology at the University of Chicago, performed one of the largest psychological studies on happiness in history. He interviewed people who spent a great amount of time and effort doing challenging work, about the times in their lives when they felt their best. He studied surgeons, professors, clerical workers, musicians, sportsmen, American assembly-line workers, Chinese cooks, Italian farmers in the Alps, Navajo sheepherders, Japanese motorcycle gang members, young European mothers, and old Asian women. He concluded, "The way a long-distance swimmer feels when crossing the English Channel was almost identical to the way a chess player feels during a tournament, or a climber progressing up a difficult rock face."

From "musicians composing a new quartet to teenagers from the ghetto involved in a championship basketball game," they all had the same inner experience, even if their activities were utterly different. Regardless of their age, culture, and country, everyone reported that they felt their best when they were in *flow*.

Flow is a state of being when we are completely focused, and fully immersed in what we are doing. In flow our work seems effortless, creativity goes into overdrive, we feel inspired, and motivation springs forth from within.

Dr. Charles Limb, surgeon and neuroscientist at the University of California in San Francisco, discovered using brain imaging technology that when we are in flow, the part of the brain responsible for self-monitoring—our inner critic—is turned off. The voices of doubt, hesitation, confusion, and worry vanish. We get out of our own way, and we are liberated from fear. We feel free.

When we are in flow, we are fully energized, we feel a deep sense of joy in every moment, and our performance skyrockets. We get so immersed in our work that nothing else seems to matter, and when we come out on the other side, we feel ecstatic about what we've done. The best moments of our lives are those when we reach beyond ourselves, live with meaning, go into the unknown with an open heart, carry the battle, and emerge successful.

Professor Csikszentmihalyi chose the term *flow* because everyone reported that the experience of flow feels "flowy." The state of flow feels flowy because love—the substance and creative power of the universe—literally flows through us. When we live in Truth, "Out of his heart will flow rivers of living water," said Jesus (John 7:38)—the spirit literally flows from within. We become a channel through which passion, purpose, and enthusiasm pour into the world.

2.

When you live in Truth, you act aligned with your mind and heart. Your body functions at optimal parameters, and your immune system is strengthened. You are serene because you don't have inner conflicts. You persist in learning, and you explore until you have the knowledge and the experience required to succeed. You do the work. You are fulfilled by the process, and by the result. You flow toward your dream, rather than pushing against it. You have the grit to cross the desert, and to suffer through the brief difficulties that show up along the way. You become independent of the social pressure, and you think for yourself. You share your work with the world, and that makes it meaningful and rewarding. You are inspired to continue. Love flows through you, and you feel free. When you live in Truth, you take risks because you know the cost of sacrificing who you are is far greater than losing money or other fleeting external possessions. You live in peace because you are fulfilling your heart's calling.

When you ignore the Truth, the mind goes against the heart, and you act against your will. Your body is knocked out of balance, and your immune system is weakened. Eventually you fall ill. Your inner conflicts tear you down, you are exhausted and burned-out. Anger, anxiety, and depression are almost certain.

You try everything—alcohol, drugs, sex, games—to avoid feeling the pain, but nothing works because Truth cannot be denied. You don't care about your work, you don't share it with others, and that makes it meaningless. You get paid to do your job, but you don't see any point in what you're doing, and it feels like a waste of time. You hate the process, and you struggle only for the outcome and the weekend. You are not willing to risk anything to give your dreams a chance, and you cling to material possessions because you think they can remove the hollowness from your heart.

When you ignore the Truth, your mind and behaviors become prisoners of the social environment. You strive to please others, to fit in and feel accepted. In spite of that, you still don't feel accepted, and not because others don't accept you, but because you haven't accepted yourself as you are. You can't stand being alone with yourself, and you feel an intolerable sense of emptiness because you have rejected the very part of yourself that gives meaning to your life: your heart. You live in fear because you are not fulfilling your calling.

3.

John Hagel, chairman of a major Silicon Valley–based research center, discovered that when you live with meaning, you unleash in your brain and body a powerful cycle that sustains you in the pursuit of dreams: *exploring* opportunities and *connecting* with like-minded people.

When you explore, you engage in creative thinking and intense ideation sessions, you solve problems and overcome challenges. Exploration is also the secret to your mind's eternal youth. No matter what age you are, when you stop learning and exploring, you begin to grow old. Reality rushes by you, and you live in the past, believing a truth that has now become a lie, and wandering around in a world that no longer exists.

When you connect, you bond with people who share your passion, you learn from each other and grow faster together. When you explore, you connect with people and form trust-based relationships. When you connect, these bonds empower you to explore greater challenges together.

The brain's two most powerful neurotransmitters—dopamine and oxytocin—are in direct relationship to the *exploration* and *connection* required in the pursuit of dreams. When you explore, the brain releases dopamine, a feel-good chemical that helps you focus your attention on the goal and gives you the energy to develop the knowledge and the skills you need to get there faster. Dopamine gives you a sense of pleasure, and increases your motivation to pursue the anticipated reward. The brain releases dopamine when you have an insight, a creative thought, when you discover the link between parallel ideas. This dopamine release expands your thinking further, so your mind spirals with one good idea leading to the next. Dopamine is associated with the process of exploration and the anticipation of reward, rather than the actual reward. Dopamine is the neurotransmitter that stimulates your thinking and keeps you doing what you love in the long run. You take risks because dopamine makes you more willing to explore new opportunities, to go beyond your comfort zone and trust the unknown. When you connect with like-minded people, the brain releases oxytocin, a neurotransmitter that gives you a calm and soothing feeling. You trust more, you have empathy and compassion, you share, and you are more generous. Bonding with others reinforces the release of oxytocin, which strengthens the human connection even further.

An extraordinary circle forms when you live with meaning. When you listen just once to the calling of your heart, you begin to focus your mind on what you love to explore. Dopamine immediately kicks in to sustain your focus over long periods of time and through increasingly challenging work. Your mind, your heart, and your actions are aligned. Even if you don't have a clue what you are doing, you connect with other people who share your passion, and you work together to reach your goals. Oxytocin rewards the human connection with feelings of trust and bonding, intimate friendships, and generosity. You feel appreciated and valued by others; you feel that you matter and that you are part of something meaningful.

The brain evolves over time and crystallizes thoughts into habits. As dopamine and oxytocin are released more often because you focus your mind on your heart's calling and you do the work, the brain becomes more efficient and sustains you to pursue your dreams further and get results faster.

Nature designed us to live in Truth, to work from love. The problems that show up for us in life are not punishments *from* nature but the consequence of us living *against* nature.

AFTERWORD

The context we live in today empowers us. Walk out in the world with a sense of hope, because the world is far better than you think, and it is only getting better. Trust science more than gossip, and make decisions about your life based on love, on your hopes, aspirations, and desires— not on worry, deceptions, and fear.

Walk outside and look around you. Realize that almost everybody is a friend. Most people are working hard to make all our lives better: the bus driver, the barista, the girl walking her dog, the businessman in a suit, the woman holding her baby, the guy with glasses. We all have divine gifts and something unique to contribute through our passion, experience, education, culture, language, and history.

Millions of people have sacrificed themselves for thousands of years so that you can be where you are today, holding this book in your hands, and having a chance to live your dreams. There's no more time to doubt; there's no more need for pain. When you close this book, you will see the world with new eyes. You are empowered from within when you now live in Truth, and you are empowered by the social environment.

What is your will in this beautiful world that's emerging? What do you will for your life? If you align your thoughts, feelings, and behaviors with love itself, divine grace will carry you through the unknown to the fulfillment of your dreams.

What matters to you? Because you cannot run away from what matters to you and expect to find happiness, peace, and meaning. There are a billion people in the world who are unfulfilled and unhappy, sad and depressed, living in pain and not caring about what they do. If you know somebody like that, give them a copy of this book to let them know they matter. The ones who change the world are people like you and me, ordinary people who live in Truth, do everyday things, and create a new destiny for themselves, even when nobody's watching. Whoever you are, wherever you are, you matter.

I love you,
Dr. Dragos

JOIN THE MOVEMENT

Let's do something great together. If you believe
everyone deserves to make their dreams a reality,
give copies of this book to your friends, follow me
at Facebook.com/DrDragosB, and join the global
conversation at #THEPURSUITOFDREAMS.

WATCH THE DOCUSERIES

Visit DrDragos.com to watch *The Pursuit of Dreams*
docuseries. Join luminaries, including Gregg Braden,
Dr. Joe Dispenza, Dr. Bruce Lipton, Dr. Peter Diamandis, and Anousheh Ansari, in this 9-episode series that
will guide you in the manifestation of *your* dreams.

WORKBOOK

Blaise Pascal, the famous mathematician and philosopher, said that there is a God-shaped hole in the heart of every person. We all, without exception, strive for happiness; however, after all the years that humankind has been on earth, we are still trying to find it. Pascal believed that this all pointed to one thing: "What is it then that this desire and this inability proclaim to us, but that there was once in man a true happiness of which there now remain to him only the mark and empty trace, which he in vain tries to fill . . ." Yet we cannot fill it with earthly matters because we will always find them inadequate. He writes, "the infinite abyss can only be filled by an infinite and immutable object, that is to say, only by God Himself."

For more than 10 years, I have been back and forth and around the world on a journey to search for that *something* that would give meaning to my life. Something that would fill that "infinite abyss" inside me. I have found it. Now I give it to you as well.

Pascal was correct in saying that the only way to fill the emptiness within—to find love, peace that transcends understanding, and a profound sense of purpose in life—is by listening to Jesus when he said: "Follow me." My dearest reader, I wasn't raised in a Christian community; I went to church only once, for Easter, every other year. I was trained as an engineer and scientist in the aerospace industry. I worked with leaders from NASA and tech entrepreneurs in Silicon Valley, and nothing in my life had prepared me for the revelations I had during my journey. I have come to know that Truth has a name: Jesus. With him, you will experience rivers of peace, forgiveness, power, and love you never knew were possible. Not with me, not with the church, not with religion, but only with him, in a personal and intimate relationship. Just as I wrote in this book, you don't need to believe a word I am saying—try it yourself. Invite him into your heart, and talk to him as you would with your dearest friend, in love, sincerity, and truth. He is the rock upon which you build your life.

Going further, if you need more concrete help in discovering your passion and making your dreams a reality, the following questions and exercises will guide you. Take a pen, and write the answers in a journal or right here in the book. Be totally honest with yourself; healing, love, and meaning await you on the other side of your embracing the Truth.

Live Your Purpose

•

What is your will in this world of abundance and possibility? What do you sincerely want to do?

You cannot lie to yourself about who you are, what you value, and what you want, and still expect to live a joyful and meaningful life. When you begin lying to yourself, you become your worst enemy because you're attacking yourself from within, and you don't stand a chance. You do not deserve that. Accepting reality, and embracing the truth in sincerity and without judgment, regardless of the fear you go through at first, is the way to peace and fulfillment.

Pick up your pen and put your hand on your heart. Breathe deeply as if you were breathing through your heart. Thank your heart, for it gives you life. Every beat of your heart is pulsing with life. Feel your heart.

Ask your heart the following questions, and when you feel the answers, acknowledge them. Honor them. Don't think too much about it; just write it down. Your heart will speak only love, meaning, and truth.

If my life ended in this moment, would I have been happy with how I've lived?

Do I really live my life from the heart, truthful about who I am?

If the answer is no, what can I do from now on to be more fulfilled with my life?

What do I really value, what do I care about? (Examples: working with children, protecting the environment, using technology to improve the lives of people, health care, bringing God back into people's lives, etc.)

What problems in the world do I want to solve or make a contribution toward solving?

What regrets do I have about my life?

How can I live from now on without accumulating even more regrets?

What contribution would I make in the world if I received a check for $1 billion?

If I came back to live another life in the future, how would I want the world to be? What contribution can I make now so that the world of the future is closer to that vision?

What impact do I want to have on the world, and on the people around me?

Before I die, I truly want to . . .

Live Your Story

•

What is my gift? What is the easiest and most natural thing for me to do (e.g., cooking, music, writing, entrepreneurship, traveling)?

What do I love to read, study, learn, and discover?

What do I do because I want to, even if I'm not being paid for it?

What brings me joy moment by moment?

Do I want to take my passion to a new level, and make it sustainable? (You might have been working on your passion for many years in your free time, but never considered the possibility of transforming it into a sustainable project or business. Don't think only about the end result, think also about the process.)

Do I honestly enjoy the process? Why? How?

Am I willing to work for years to make my dreams come true?

How can I transform my gift into a product or service that makes the lives of others better?

What is the most beautiful story I can tell about my product or service?

How does it bring more joy, more health, more love, more peace in the world?

Tell your story. Tell your unique story. Believe your story. Live the story.

Live the Grace

•

Almost every personal-development book on the shelves speaks about the power of gratitude. I want you to go a step further and realize that nothing is as important as—and nothing deserves your appreciation, love, and gratitude as much as—the people in your life.

Put your hand on your heart. Breathe deeply, as if you were breathing through your heart. Feel your heart, then answer the following questions.

Who in my life makes me feel happiest?

Who in my life makes me feel richest?

Who in my life makes me feel most loved?

What do I feel happiest about?

I will appreciate these people tonight: [write the names of each person, and the specific reasons you appreciate them].

If you live in a context in which expressing authentic appreciation is not common, you might find it difficult to do it verbally. You must rise above the environment to live your heart's calling. If you cannot say it, send an e-mail, write a letter, leave a message—just do it!

Keep All Agreements

•

What agreements do I have with myself about my life?

What agreements do I have with my family?

Do I keep my agreements with myself? What agreements have I broken and must I honor?

Do I keep my promises with my family? What agreements have I broken and must I honor?

Do I keep my promises about my work? Do I always deliver the work, as I promise?

Rise above the Line of Supercredibility

•

The best way to go above the line of supercredibility is to surround yourself with people who create a highly credible environment.

Who can I invite today to join my project or business who will offer me supercredibility?

What can I offer them? Why should they join me?

How will they benefit from joining my project? (Most likely they don't need and won't ask for money.) Can I offer them a way to make a contribution to society?

Embrace the Uncomfortable Reality

•

The only way to solve the problems in your life is to do something that is very unnatural for people to do: define and accept reality. Face the problems, and deal with them head-on. Most people either lie to themselves about their problems or make them much worse and lose their power to make a change. Addressing the uncomfortable reality is hard because fear creeps in. Until you accept your fears, you cannot overcome them, and until you embrace your demons, you cannot heal them. You don't run from fear; you go through fear.

My unpleasant reality is: [for example, I am in the wrong job, I don't really care about my work, I put my work far above my family and health, I am in the wrong relationship, I am not happy where I am, I don't live what I really value, I don't have the confidence that my dreams are possible].

100 Percent Commitment

•

The main thing in my life that from now on comes above everything else is:

From now on, I am 100 percent committed to making a change in my life. What action must I take now?

100 Percent Accountability

•

I understand that I am solely accountable to live in Truth, make my dreams a reality, and live the life I want. Drama never gets me anywhere, and there is nobody to blame and nothing to complain about. If I want to live a great life, I need to be fully accountable for my future, regardless of the social environment, the circumstances, or how difficult the journey may be. I will honor love. I will live my truth, starting now.

Sign your name below:

Now go do it.

BIBLIOGRAPHY

Foreword

Rizzolatti, Giacomo, and Laila Craighero. "The Mirror Neuron System" (PDF). *Annual Review of Neuroscience* 27, no. 1 (2004):169–192.

A Note from the Author

The Holy Bible, King James Version (KJV). Public domain. Retrieved from: http://www.biblegateway.com.

Chapter 3

Allen, Lew. *The Hubble Space Telescope Optical Systems Failure Report*. NASA Technical Report NASA-TM-103443, November 1, 1990. https://ntrs.nasa.gov/search.jsp?R=19910003124.

Asch, Solomon. "Effects of Group Pressure on the Modification and Distortion of Judgments." In *Groups, Leadership and Men*, edited by H. Guetzkow. Pittsburgh, PA: Carnegie Press, 1951.

———. "Opinions and Social Pressure." *Scientific American* 193, no. 5 (1955):31–35.

———. *Social Psychology*. Englewood Cliffs, NJ: Prentice Hall, 1952.

ASK Magazine Staff. "ASK Talks with Dr. Charles Pellerin." *APPL: The NASA Academy of Program and Project Leadership*, August 1, 2013. https://appel.nasa.gov/2003/08/01/ask-talks-with-dr -charles-pellerin.

Blakeslee, Sandra. "What Other People Say May Change What You See." *The New York Times*, June 28, 2005. http://www .nytimes.com/2005/06/28/science/what-other-people-say-may -change-what-you-see.html.

Dick, Steven J., ed. *NASA's First 50 Years: Historical Perspectives*. Washington, DC: Superintendent of Documents, U.S. Government Printing Office, 2009. https://www.nasa.gov/connect /ebooks/hist_nasa50_detail.html.

Johnson, Stephen B. "Success, Failure and NASA Culture." *NASA ASK Magazine* 5, no. 1 (1 Sept 2008). https://appel.nasa.gov /2008/09/01/success-failure-and-nasa-culture.

National Geographic. *Air Crash Investigation: Ripped from the Cockpit*.

Pellerin, Charles. *How NASA Builds Teams: Mission Critical Soft Skills for Scientists, Engineers and Project Managers*. Hoboken, NJ: Wiley, 2008.

Rhoda, D. A., and M. L. Pawlak. "An Assessment of Thunderstorm Penetrations and Deviations by Commercial Aircraft in the Terminal Area." Lincoln Laboratory, Massachusetts Institute of Technology, June 3, 1999. https://www.ll.mit.edu/mission /aviation/publications/publication-files/nasa-reports/Rhoda _1999_NASA-A2_WW-10087.pdf.

Rogers, William P., et al. *Report of the Presidential Commission on the Space Shuttle Challenger Accident*, 1986. https://history.nasa .gov/rogersrep/genindex.htm.

Vaughan, Diane. *The Challenger Launch Decision: Risky Technology, Culture and Deviance at NASA*. Chicago: University of Chicago Press, 1996.

Zimmerman, Robert. *The Universe in a Mirror: The Saga of the Hubble Space Telescope and the Visionaries Who Built it*. Princeton, NJ: Princeton University Press, 2008.

Chapter 4

Alexander, Bruce. *Addiction: The View from Rat Park*. http://www
.brucekalexander.com/articles-speeches/rat-park/148-addiction
-the-view-from-rat-park.

―――. "The Effect of Housing and Gender on Morphine
Self-Administration in Rats." *Psychopharmacology* 58, no. 2 (6 Jul
1978):175–179.

―――. *The Globalization of Addiction: A Study in the Poverty of
Spirit*. Oxford: Oxford University Press, 2008.

―――. *The Rise and Fall of the Official View on Addiction*. July 3,
2014. http://www.brucekalexander.com/articles-speeches/277
-rise-and-fall-of-the-official-view-of-addiction-6.

Alexander, Bruce, et al. "Effect of Early and Later Colony Housing on Oral Ingestion of Morphine in Rats." *Pharmacology,
Biochemistry and Behaviour* 15, no. 4 (Oct 1981):571–76.

Cohen, Peter. *The Naked Empress: Modern Neuroscience and the
Concept of Addiction*. Presentation at the 12th Platform for Drug
Treatment, Mondsee Austria, 21–22 March 2009. Organized by
the Österreichische Gesellschaft für arzneimittelgestützte Be-
handlung von Suchtkranken OEGABS. http://www.cedro-uva
.org/lib/cohen.empress.html.

Frankl, Viktor E. *Man's Search for Meaning*. Boston: Beacon Press,
1959.

Hari, Johann. *Chasing the Scream*. New York: Bloomsbury, 2015.

Nag Hammadi Library. *The Book of Thomas the Contender*. Translated by John D. Turner. The Gnostic Society Library. http://
gnosis.org/naghamm/bookt.html.

―――. *The Gospel of Thomas*. Translated by Stephen Patterson
and Marvin Meyer. The Gnostic Society Library. http://gnosis
.org/naghamm/gosthom.html.

Reding, Nick. *Methland: The Death and Life of an American Small
Town*. New York: Bloomsbury, 2009.

Robbins, Lee N. "Vietnam Veterans' Rapid Recovery from Heroin Addiction: A Fluke or Normal Expectation?" *Addiction* 88 (1993):1041–1054. http://www.rkp.wustl.edu/VESlit/Robins Addiction1993.pdf.

Slater, Lauren. *Opening Skinner's Box: Great Psychological Experiments of the Twentieth Century.* New York: Norton, 2005.

Warner, Jessica. *Craze: Gin and Debauchery in an Age of Reason.* New York: Four Walls Eight Windows, 2002.

Zinberg, Norman E. "Heroin Use in Vietnam and the United States: A Contrast and a Critique." *Archives of General Psychiatry* 26, no. 5 (1972):486–488.

Chapter 5

Altman, Lawrence K. "U.S. Scientist Wins Nobel for Controversial Work." *The New York Times*, October 7, 1997. http://www.nytimes.com/1997/10/07/us/us-scientist-wins-nobel-for-controversial-work.html.

Dao, James, and Andrew W. Lehren. "Baffling Rise in Suicides Plagues the U.S. Military," *The New York Times*, May 15, 2013. http://www.nytimes.com/2013/05/16/us/baffling-rise-in-suicides-plagues-us-military.html.

The Holy Bible, American Standard Version (ASV). Public domain. Retrieved from: http://www.biblegateway.com.

Nicks, Denver. "Suicide Rate Soars among Young Vets," *Time Magazine*, January 10, 2014. http://time.com/304/report-suicide-rate-soars-among-young-vets.

Pilkington, Ed. "U.S. Military Struggling to Stop Suicide Epidemic among War Veterans," *The Guardian*, February 1, 2013. https://www.theguardian.com/world/2013/feb/01/us-military-suicide-epidemic-veteran.

The Planetary Society. "A Pale Blue Dot." http://www.planetary.org/explore/space-topics/earth/pale-blue-dot.html.

Sagan, Carl. "Wonder and Skepticism." *Skeptical Inquirer* 19.1 (Jan/Feb 1995). https://www.csicop.org/si/show/wonder_and_skepticism.

Zimbardo, Philip. *The Lucifer Effect: Understanding How Good People Turn Evil.* New York: Random House, 2007.

Chapter 7

al-Din Rumi, Jalal. *The Essential Rumi.* New York: HarperCollins, 1995.

Amundsen, Roald. *My Life as an Explorer.* Cambridge: Cambridge University Press, 1927.

———. *The South Pole: An Account of the Norwegian Antarctic Expedition in the "Fram" 1910–1912.* London: J. Murray, 1913.

Niederkorn, William S. "'I Have the Pole,' Robert E. Peary Wires." *The New York Times,* September 7, 2009. https://times traveler.blogs.nytimes.com/2009/09/07/i-have-the-pole-robert -e-peary-wires.

Sandwell, Ruth, and John Lutz. "The Franklin Mystery: Life and Death in the Arctic." http://www.canadianmysteries.ca/sites /franklin/home/homeIntro_en.htm

Solomon, Andrew. *The Noonday Demon: An Atlas on Depression.* New York: Simon and Schuster, 2001.

Woodman, David C. *Unravelling the Franklin Mystery: Inuit Testimony.* Montreal: McGill-Queen's Press, 1992.

Chapter 8

Cialdini, Robert. *Influence: The Psychology of Persuasion.* New York: Collins Business Essentials, 1993.

CVR transcript American Flight 1420, June 1, 1999: https:// aviation-safety.net/investigation/cvr/transcripts/cvr_aa1420.php.

Federal Aviation Administration. "American Airlines Flight 1420, MD-82, N215AA." http://lessonslearned.faa.gov/ll_main .cfm?TabID=1&LLID=61&LLTypeID=0.

National Geographic. *Air Crash Investigation: Racing the Storm.*

Chapter 9

Belohlavek, Peter, and John W. Wagner. *Innovation: The Lessons of Nikola Tesla*. Chestnut Ridge, NY: Blue Eagle Group, 2008.

Ekman, Paul. *Emotions Revealed, Second Edition: Recognizing Faces and Feelings to Improve Communication and Emotional Life*. New York: Owl Books, 2003.

———. *Is Love an Emotion?* Paul Ekman Group, November 11, 2015. http://www.paulekman.com/psychology/is-love-an-emotion.

Gyatso, Venerable Geshe Kelsang. "What Is the Mind?" Kadampa Buddhism. http://kadampa.org/reference/mind.

HeartMath Institute. *You Can Change Your DNA*. HeartMath Institute, July 14, 2011. https://www.heartmath.org/articles-of -the-heart/personal-development/you-can-change-your-dna.

Helps Ministries. "Nous." HELPS Word-studies. http://biblehub .com/greek/3563.htm.

Hoffman, Kent. "Every Person Has Infinite Worth | Kent Hoffman | TEDxSpokane." Posted to YouTube by TEDx Talks, November 25, 2015. https://youtu.be/E9fHCrP8hZM.

The Holy Bible, World English Bible. Public domain. Retrieved from: http://www.biblegateway.com.

Maksimov, Deacon George. "Three-Hundred Sayings of the Ascetics of the Orthodox Church." http://orthodox.cn/patristics /300sayings_en.htm.

McCraty, Rollin, Mike Atkinson, and Dana Tomasino. "Modulation of DNA Conformation by Heart-Focused Intention." HeartMath Research Center, Institute of HeartMath, Publication No. 03-008, 2003. http://www.aipro.info/drive/File/224.pdf.

Merriam-Webster. "Mind." Merriam-Webster.com. https://www .merriam-webster.com/dictionary/mind.

Nag Hammadi Library. *The Gospel of Thomas*. Translated by Stephen Patterson and Marvin Meyer. The Gnostic Society Library. http://gnosis.org/naghamm/gosthom.html.

Oxford University Press. "Mind." Oxford Living Dictionaries. https://en.oxforddictionaries.com/definition/mind.

Schrijver, Karel, and Iris Schrijver. *Living with the Stars: How the Human Body Is Connected to the Life Cycles of the Earth, the Planets and the Stars.* Oxford: Oxford University Press, 2015.

Worrall, Simon. "How 40,000 Tons of Cosmic Dust Falling to Earth Affects You and Me." *National Geographic*, January 28, 2015. http://news.nationalgeographic.com/2015/01/150128-big-bang-universe-supernova-astrophysics-health-space-ngbooktalk.

Chapter 10

Amundsen, Roald. *My Life as an Explorer.* Cambridge: Cambridge University Press, 1927.

———. *The South Pole: An Account of the Norwegian Antarctic Expedition in the "Fram" 1910–1912.* London: J. Murray, 1913.

Burkeman, Oliver. *The Antidote: Happiness for People Who Can't Stand Positive Thinking.* New York: Farrar, Straus and Giroux, 2012.

Ellis, Albert. *How to Stubbornly Refuse to Make Yourself Miserable about Anything: Yes, Anything.* New York: Citadel Press, 2006.

Hamilton, Allan J. *The Scalpel and the Soul: Encounters with Surgery, the Supernatural, and the Healing Power of Hope.* New York: Tarcher/Penguin, 2008.

Holmes, Oliver Wendell. *Elsie Venner.* Boston: Tickner and Fields, 1861.

Chapter 12

Diamandis, Peter, and Steven Kotler. *Bold: How to Go Big, Create Wealth and Impact the World.* New York: Simon and Schuster, 2015.

Giroux, Joan. *The Haiku Form.* Tokyo: Charles E. Tuttle, 1974.

Chapter 14

The Holy Bible, World English Bible. Public domain. Retrieved from: http://www.biblegateway.com.

Chapter 15

Alsop, Ronald. *Instant Gratification and Its Dark Side*. Bucknell University, July 17, 2014. http://www.bucknell.edu/communications /bucknell-magazine/instant-gratification-and-its-dark-side.html.

Common Sense Media. *Children, Teens and Entertainment Media: View from the Classroom Final Report*. 2012. https://www.common sensemedia.org/file/view-from-the-classroom-final-reportpdf-0 /download.

Gilbert, Daniel T., Romin W. Tafarodi, and Patrick S. Malone. "You Can't Not Believe Everything You Read." *Journal of Personality and Social Psychology* 65, no. 2 (2003):221–223.

Gilovich, Thomas, Dale Griffin, and Daniel Kahneman, eds. *Heuristics and Biases: The Psychology of Intuitive Judgment*. Cambridge: Cambridge University Press, 2002.

Worthy, Darrell, Marissa Gorlick, Jose Pacheco, David Schnyer, and Todd Maddox. "With Age Comes Wisdom: Decision-Making in Younger and Older Adults." *Psychological Science* 22 (2011):1375–1380.

Chapter 16

D'Onfro, Jillian. "How Jack Ma Went from Being a Poor School Teacher to Turning Alibaba into a $160 Billion Behemoth." *Business Insider*, September 14, 2014. http://www.businessinsider .com/the-story-of-jack-ma-founder-of-alibaba-2014-9.

Gladwell, Malcolm. *Outliers: The Story of Success*. New York: Hachette, 2008.

Jackson, Laura. *Jon Bon Jovi: The Biography*. New York: Hachette, 2003.

Morais, Fernando. *Paulo Coelho: A Warrior's Life: The Authorized Biography*. New York: HarperCollins, 2010.

Mother Teresa. *Come Be My Light: The Private Writings of the Saint of Calcutta*. Edited by Brian Kolodiejchuk. New York: Doubleday, 2007.

"Mother Teresa of Calcutta." The Holy See. http://www.vatican.va/news_services/liturgy/saints/ns_lit_doc_20031019_madre-teresa_en.html.

Naipaul, V. S. *A Bend in the River*. New York: Knopf, 1979.

Tagore, Rabindranath. *Fruit Gathering*. New York: Macmillan, 1916.

Wadhwa, Vivek. "The Case for Old Entrepreneurs." *Washington Post*, December 2, 2011. http://wadhwa.com/2011/12/02/washington-post-the-case-for-old-entrepreneurs.

Winfrey, Oprah. "Oprah Learns the Secret to Paulo Coelho's Timeless Wisdom." Oprah.com, October 2014. http://www.oprah.com/inspiration/oprah-talks-to-the-alchemist-author-paulo-coelho.

Zappa, Frank. *Frank Zappa and the Mother of Invention: One Size Fits All*. Victoria, Australia: Hal Leonard, 1975.

Chapter 18

Diamandis, Peter. *Abundance: The Future Is Better than You Think*. New York: Free Press, 2014.

———. "The 'Rising Billion' New Consumers Will Arrive by 2020." *The World Post*. https://www.huffingtonpost.com/peter-diamandis/rising-billion-consumers_b_7008160.html.

The Economist. "Toward the End of Poverty." *The Economist*, June 1, 2013. http://www.economist.com/news/leaders/21578665-nearly-1-billion-people-have-been-taken-out-extreme-poverty-20-years-world-should-aim.

Kurzweil, Ray. *The Age of Spiritual Machines*. New York: Viking Press, 1999.

———. "How My Predictions Are Faring." October 2010. http://www.kurzweilai.net/images/How-My-Predictions-Are-Faring.pdf

———. *The Singularity Is Near*. New York: Penguin, 2005.

Pressfield, Steven. *The War of Art: Break Through the Blocks and Win Your Inner Creative Battles*. New York: Black Irish Entertainment, 2002.

Chapter 19

The Holy Bible, World English Bible. Public domain. Retrieved from: http://www.biblegateway.com.

Chapter 20

Csikszentmihalyi, Mihaly. *Flow: The Psychology of Happiness: The Classic Work on How to Achieve Happiness.* New York: Random House, 1994.

Hagel, John. *Passion and Plasticity—The Neurobiology of Passion.* January 18, 2011. Edge Perspectives with John Hagel. http://edgeperspectives.typepad.com/edge_perspectives/2011/01/passion-and-plasticity-the-neurobiology-of-passion.html.

The Holy Bible, New King James Version. Nashville, TN: Thomas Nelson, 1982. Retrieved from: http://www.biblegateway.com.

Kotler, Steven. *The Rise of Superman: Decoding the Science of Optimal Performance.* London: Quercus, 2014.

Limb, Charles. "Your Brain on Improv." TED Talk, November 2010. https://www.ted.com/talks/charles_limb_your_brain_on_improv?language=en.

Workbook

Pascal, Blaise. *Pascal's Pensées.* New York: E. P. Dutton & Co., Inc., 1958. Archived by Project Gutenberg, April 27, 2006. http://www.gutenberg.org/files/18269/18269-h/18269-h.htm.

Other Resources Consulted

Schuchman, Helen. *A Course in Miracles.* New York: Viking Foundation for Inner Peace, 1976.

Szekely, Edmond Bordeaux. *The Essene Gospel of Peace.* USA: International Biogenic Society, 1971.

ACKNOWLEDGMENTS

These pages are my opportunity to express my thankfulness for those I have shared the journey with, and I would like to start with you, my dear reader. I appreciate you, and I love you. I am honored by your trust in me to buy this book. I hope it serves you well.

I am grateful—in spirit and in truth—to our Heavenly Father. Thank you for choosing me to bring this message to the world. After 33 years of life, I have come to know that all good in life comes from God. I thank you for my life, for all your gifts, and for your infinite love for me. I love you, Father.

I am on my knees, with arms wide open in gratitude, to Jesus Christ, my savior and my lord. I am grateful and honored to serve you with my everything. I know that without your love, humanity would be slogging through the darkness; but with your love and sacrifice, we can move the mountains. I love you, Jesus.

I honor and thank from the deepest part of my being the Holy Spirit for the inspiration and the revelation he abundantly offers me. Thank you for your perfect wisdom and gentle love. I love you, Holy Spirit.

I am grateful to my beautiful parents for their unconditional love, continuous support, and sacrifice throughout my entire life. You are the most amazing parents in the world. Everything I am, I owe to you. You have loved and nourished me since I was only a thought in the mind of God and a seed in your womb. Thank you for believing in me even when you do not understand me. I thank you, and I love you.

I am grateful to Anca for her unconditional love and infinite patience throughout the years. We've been together through the low and the high, the not-so-good and the great. You stayed with me during my worst and my best. I thank you, and I love you. You really are the light of my world.

I bow my head in thankfulness to Dr. Charles Ndifon of Christ Love Ministries International, my spiritual father; and to Gregg Braden, my beloved role model. My dreams would not have been possible without your continuous inspiration and profound wisdom. I thank both of you for your genius and your love for people. Gregg and Charles, you are precious jewels in our world. I love you both to life, and I am honored by your trust in me. Thank you!

In addition, I extend a warm and genuine thank-you to Gregg for the valuable contribution of the Foreword of the book. You have made my dream a reality.

I give infinite thanks to the most amazing group of people I could ever imagine working with: the Hay House family.

I am incredibly grateful to Nicolette Salamanca Young, my brilliant, beautiful, and extraordinary editor who transforms pages of text into masterpieces of literary wisdom. I thank you for your trust in me, and for bringing your magic touch to this book. I am looking forward to seeing where this journey takes us together in the years to come.

To Louise Hay: I never had the chance to meet you in person, but I honor you for having been a bright light in our world.

To Reid Tracy and Patty Gift: Thank you for trusting me with this book and for giving me such a warm welcome into the Hay House family. I appreciate you for your genius and for your giant, beautiful hearts. I hope we will have another 100 years together on this journey.

To Tricia Breidenthal and Caroline DiNofia: Thank you for your beautiful genius and inspiration in designing the cover of this book.

I give thanks to every single team member at Hay House for your dedication and hard work to bring more hope, healing, and joy to our world. I appreciate you and love you all dearly.

The writing of this book is only the first step in the process that takes it from my laptop into your hands. Along the way, copy editors, proofreaders, graphic designers, marketing representatives, publicists, event producers, and bookstore buyers have made incredibly valuable contributions to make this book a reality. Although I will never meet most of these people personally, I know they're there. I honor each one of you for your dedication to bringing this book to people. Your work truly matters. I thank you, and I love you.

I am grateful to my extraordinary production team who worked hard for many months to create *The Pursuit of Dreams* docuseries: Anca Turtica, the divinely inspired writer of the series; Andrei Stan, the exceptionally talented director and movie editor; Andrei Ceobanu, the remarkable editor and graphic designer; and Andrei Tatu, the genius behind the soundboard. Thank you for being there for me every time I called you. Very special thanks to our beautiful and brilliant web developer, Nicolette Marais. To Cristian, Ciprian, and the entire team at Soft-Expert Mobility: Thank you for your trust, patience and professional savvy with developing the Amazing University mobile app.

I acknowledge and honor the following people who've entered my life as the divine solution to prayers: Dorin Prunariu; Monica Visan; Mona Taponen and Andrea Balzarini; Mark Johnson and Ryan Hendrickson; Daniel and Simona Mironescu; Natalia and Mircea Volosen; Ed and Deb Shapiro; Ellen Fisk; Andrea Collura; Bernice Collura; Steven Jacquier and Doran Vaughan; Irma Bonniot; Sylvia Vowless; Teresa Valenzuela; Karin Lewis and Warner Lewis III; Karen Koebnick; Jerry Miner; Joyce Hrstich; Martha Reich Braden; Gary and Raywyn Cook; Cristi Turtica; Gordon Roberts and Heidi Wozny; Einstein and Christine Ntim; Guy Djoken; Mike Bull; Ann Russell; Dr. Maureen Hoyt and the leadership team at the Centers for Spiritual Living; Yoko Yuile Shinoda; Teo, Nina, and Eliza Biris; Gec Diaconu; Octavian Baban; Catalin Raceanu; Stefan Dan; Razvan Dimitriu; Fatima Verissimo; and Emanuel Dumitrescu.

To all, I am forever grateful.

ABOUT THE AUTHOR

Dr. Dragos Bratasanu is an award-winning scientist, author, filmmaker, and speaker who has presented on five continents. He is the founder of Amazing University, a mobile app available on iOS and Android, with online courses that have inspired numerous people in 56 countries.

Dr. Dragos holds a Ph.D. in the field of satellite-based intelligence from the University of Siegen, Germany, and has received several international awards for his scientific innovation. In his 20s, Dragos traveled on two expeditions to the North and the South Poles, and was the engineer and journalist of a simulation mission for Mars. His team at Singularity University was named by *Forbes* magazine "among the smartest people in the world," and Dragos was nominated for the M.I.T. list of Innovators Under 35—a prestigious recognition for "the brightest minds in Europe who are changing society."

Dr. Dragos's movie *The Amazing You* was translated into 20 languages, was declared one of the "Top 10 Independent Films that Could Change the World" by Life Changes Network, and received the "Award of Merit for Education" from the Accolade Global Film Competition. With *The Pursuit of Dreams* book, Dr. Dragos also released

The Pursuit of Dreams docuseries, available on his website and in stores.

Dr. Dragos now travels the world to empower people to make their dreams a reality anywhere they start, and to bring us back to God—the only place where we find healing, forgiveness, purpose, and love.

Visit his official website at www.drdragos.com.